# CREATING
# ROOMS OF WONDER

CAROL SEEFELDT

# Dedication

*Creating Rooms of Wonder* is dedicated to Kathy Charner, editor extraordinaire.

# Creating Rooms of Wonder

## Valuing and Displaying Children's Work to Enhance the Learning Process

**Carol Seefeldt**
Illustrated by Joan Waites

gryphon house®, inc.
Beltsville, MD 20704

## Copyright

## Library of Congress Cataloging-in-Publication Data

Seefeldt, Carol.
    Creating rooms of wonder : valuing and displaying children's work to enhance
the learning process / Carol Seefeldt; illustrated by Joan Waites.
        p.cm.
Includes bibliographical references and index.
    ISBN 0-87659-265-5
    1. Displays in education—Handbooks, manuals, etc.  2. Early childhood
education—Handbooks, manuals, etc.  I. Title.
LB1043.6 .S44 2002
371.33'56--dc21

2002006950

## Bulk Purchase

## Disclaimer

# Table of Contents

# Preface

## Creating Rooms of Wonder

*Creating Rooms of Wonder* offers teachers of two- to eight-year-olds a primer of how to display children's work and evidence of their thematic learning and project work. When children's work is displayed with care and thoughtfulness in childcare settings, preschools, kindergartens, and the primary grades it affirms children and their work, beautifies their surroundings, and communicates to others what children are learning and how they are developing and growing.

Because of its practicality, *Creating Rooms of Wonder* is a book teachers will be able to use every day. Offering hundreds of ideas for arranging and displaying children's art and other work, teachers will find the book of immediate and long-term usefulness. Many of the ideas presented in the book were tested during workshops with teachers of young children across the nation. Teachers at the Center for Young Children at the University of Maryland implemented a number of the ideas the day after a workshop. Over the course of a year, they found that appealing displays of children's art, thematic work, or project work increased children's feelings of self-worth and served to communicate to busy families and the university community what children do while in child care.

*Creating Rooms of Wonder* evolved from a number of experiences. First, my early educational experiences as a student teacher focused on room arrangement and the learning environment. This was when the dominant theories of children's learning were maturational. These theories led to the concept that children learned through an environment arranged specifically for them. Next were my experiences in the British Infant Schools of England and a visit to the childcare centers in Reggio Emilia, Italy. These programs both focused on surrounding children with a learning environment that communicated what they were doing and learning, and were astonishingly beautiful. In fact, the attention that the childcare centers in Reggio Emilia have received can be attributed, at least in part, to the aesthetic, even stunning displays and documentation of children's work. Everywhere you look in the centers of Reggio, children's work is beautifully displayed. Some is highlighted on discarded, lit x-ray viewers, other work is mounted under Plexiglas in hallways and the room, some hangs from the ceiling, and still more work is displayed on tables.

Given the drive in America to replicate Reggio's childcare programs, it seemed appropriate to think and write about the importance of displaying children's work in ways that affirm children, beautify their world, and communicate to others how children learn.

*Creating Rooms of Wonder* begins with an introductory chapter followed by a chapter on the basics of display. Subsequent chapters focus on framing and mounting children's work, using tabletops and shelves as foundations for displays, creating interactive bulletin boards, using graphs and surveys, constructing islands of beauty, and labeling displays.

# Chapter 1

# The ABC's of Displaying Children's Work

"Look what I made!" four-year-old Shawna said to her grandmother, pointing to a painting on the wall outside her classroom. "It's a picture of you. It says, 'I love you,'" continued Shawna. As all young children, Shawna felt valued and affirmed when she saw her work displayed in the school. It filled her with pride and gave her another way to communicate her love to her grandmother.

Displaying children's work with thoughtfulness and care has many benefits. Not just for children who know they and their creations are respected when their work is displayed, but for teachers, families, and the total early childhood program.

By displaying children's work, teachers:
- affirm children's thoughts, ideas, and imaginations
- beautify their world
- communicate to others
- document what children learn and
- extend and expand children's learning

# Affirm Children's Thoughts, Ideas, and Imaginations

Displaying children's work dignifies and recognizes the value of children's expression of their thoughts, ideas, and imaginations. Clearly, affirming, valuing, and dignifying children's work starts long before children produce a finished product. Affirmation begins by giving children time, freedom, appropriate materials, and guidance with which to express themselves freely and creatively.

Affirmation continues as teachers talk with children about what they are making and doing. Instead of saying "What a lovely painting," which is meaningless, teachers take the time to actually describe each individual child's work. "The bright green you used here stands out." "This line goes from the top of your painting all the way through to the bottom." "Look at the way the pink lightens this part of your drawing."

Likewise, project and thematic work is discussed with children in a thoughtful, focused way. Children's ideas are expanded, extended, and clarified. "Let's find a book about spiders. Then we can see how many legs a spider has." They are asked to think of alternative ways of working, "Have you thought about what would happen if you put a block here?" And children are listened to. "I understand the clay feels good in your hands."

Treating children's products with respect continues by providing children with access to places to hang wet paintings or store other work before taking it home. Then, with sensitivity to children's feelings about their work, samples are displayed in the room, hallways, and throughout the school.

Young two- and three-year-olds, who are more interested in the process of creating art and other work, are not terribly interested in the products they produce. They may not notice or care if you keep one or two of their paintings or other work to display. Their parents and others in the school, however, will want to see and know about what the two- and three-year-old children are doing and learning when in the center.

By the time children are four years old, they become possessive of their work and want to take it home with them immediately. When this happens you can create temporary display spaces where children can hang or display their work until they are ready to go home. Eventually though, children will take pride in having their work displayed so others in the room and school can enjoy it as well.

# Beautify Children's World

Children, who are innately beautiful themselves, deserve to be surrounded with beauty whether in a childcare center, preschool, kindergarten or primary grade. Displays, not only of children's written and creative products, but of their ongoing thematic and project work, serve to beautify their lives.

Because the environment affects children's behaviors, as well as their art and written work, every place children look they should see something of beauty. Arrange spaces to hold visual appeal to both children and the adults who work with them.

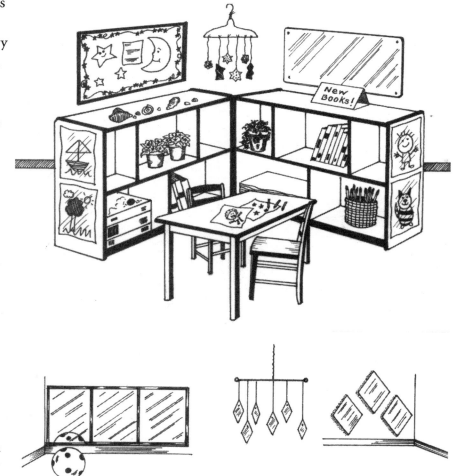

Mirrors of all types can be placed throughout the center. Hang bits of mirrors and colored glass from the ceilings to catch a sunbeam and bounce it back to the children. Mount long horizontal mirrors near the floor so children can watch themselves and others. Or attach square or triangular pieces of mirrors to other places on the walls.

Even art supplies, arranged with aesthetics in mind, are stunning works of art themselves. Arrange paints and papers by color, size, or texture, or found objects such as leaves, acorns, shells, rocks, pebbles, or feathers by color within children's reach.

In Reggio Emilia, a town in northern Italy noted for its outstanding childcare centers, children's work is another source of beauty. These displays, which include large photographs of children creating art or taking part in thematic or project work, are arranged in ways that beautify the room. Colored cloth draped over tables highlights children's sculptures and other three-dimensional work. Paintings and other two-dimensional works are mounted and displayed on contrasting paper of differing colors, textures, and prints. Printed descriptions of children at work or of their finished products are stunningly beautiful themselves.

Works of beauty in and of themselves, the displays of children's work in Reggio Emilia stimulate children to think about and reflect on past experiences and motivate them to express new and current ideas and experiences.

## Communicate to Others

Displaying children's work is a form of communication. First, displays, along with labels describing children's work, give children the idea that meaning can be shared and gained through pictures and print. Shawna demonstrated that meaning is communicated through pictures when she told her grandmother that her painting said, "I love you!"

Displays of art, thematic, and project work also give children something to talk about. Looking at displays of their work, children pick out their own work and that of others. They begin to recognize individual differences in their work and the work of others. Together they chat about how they painted their pictures and recall the theme or project they were working on at the time.

Displays of completed and ongoing work make children aware of the meaning of making pictures and print, and allow others in the school to learn from displays. Older children enjoy looking at the work of the "little kids" and reminiscing about when "they were little." The teachers of older children also benefit from viewing displays of children's work. The displays show how young children learn, helping teachers begin to learn about the children they may one day teach. The displays also show the unique way each child expresses his or her ideas, feelings, and imagination.

Parents especially benefit from seeing their children's work displayed. The displays help parents understand and respect the work of their children. Without labeled displays parents might not fully recognize the importance of scribbles, random drawings, and the seemingly abstractness of children's paintings. Written explanations that these scribbles are the beginning of writing letters and other symbols, inform and reassure parents that their children are learning.

"I am learning to write"    Juan /May 2

# Document What Children Learn

Today, society demands accountability, and children's growth, development, and learning are no exception. Appropriate displays of children's work can serve to account for, or document what children are learning, as well as how they are growing and developing.

When children's work is displayed, everyone in the school, including school administrators and others, understands better what children are doing and learning while in the classroom. When the displays are clearly labeled, over time they can become a means of authentic evaluation for administrators and others. The progress children make, the increased complexity of their projects and themes, and the increasing sophistication of children's pictorial and written expression is obvious.

# Extend and Expand Children's Learning

Displays of children's work enable children to expand and extend their hands-on project and thematic work with additional experiences. A book or two about trucks propped open under a display of children's drawings of trucks entices children to learn more about trucks as they look at drawings and photographs of trucks they haven't actually observed.

Some displays are designed to extend and expand children's knowledge through active participation. A table of rocks or shells for children to handle and sort by size, shape, color, or type provides an opportunity for children to expand their classification skills. A flannel board display with cutouts of a favorite story helps children understand story structure, and a bulletin board with the first parts of a story depicted with room for children to draw their ideas of an ending develops children's skills of predicting and concluding.

Other displays raise questions. A board may be arranged in a way that asks children to match adult animals to the baby with a piece of yarn. Another might ask children to find out which of the items depicted on the board and found on a table under the board weigh the most.

## In Summary

Thoughtfully displaying children's art products and other work is important for a number of reasons. First, displays surround children with beauty that they themselves have created.

Next, how children's first expressions—no matter how primitive—are treated will determine, in part, how children feel about themselves and how freely and fully they will be able to express themselves through a variety of media in the future. When children know their ideas and their work are valued, they are affirmed. They know they can achieve.

Displays serve to extend and expand children's project work and explorations of their world. Information in the form of photographs, pictures, or real objects added to a display reinforces children's learning and motivates them to learn still more.

Well-displayed work informs others about early childhood education. What and how young children are learning becomes more clear to parents, administrators, and other adults when they can view, handle, and read about what children are doing and learning in the early childhood program.

Even so, displays are primarily for children. Displaying children's work gives them a chance to think about their past. As they look at and handle a display, children can reflect and reminisce. They have the opportunity to talk and think about their work in the past and make plans for future work.

## Assessing Your Ideas of Displaying Children's Work

Can you recall any of your early educational experiences? I can recall building with blocks on a sunny spot on the floor when I was in kindergarten. After my friend and I had finished building a truly lovely castle, the teacher made a "Do Not Disturb" sign. She said she would show the building to the afternoon class, and when we returned the next morning, we could continue our building. Over 60 years later, I can still recall my joy and happiness of having my work affirmed!

Do you recall any memories of having your work recognized through display? How did you feel when your work was recognized? Do you have any lingering impressions of the room environment?

Use the following questions to survey and evaluate the displays in your classroom:

- How do you recognize and affirm children's work?
- Do children recognize that their work is being given special attention?
- Do they use the displays to talk about the things they've done and still want to do?
- Are your displays attractive to adults? (In Reggio Emilia many of the displays are arranged specifically for adults.)
- How do parents and other administrators treat the displays?
- Are displays attractive? How often are they changed?
- Which displays and areas of the room are attractive to you, the children, and other adults?
- Which displays do you think could be enhanced, and how?

As you read this book, make notes about the things you will try in your room. After you make changes, observe the children and note if changes in displays make a difference to the children and the group as a whole.

# Chapter 2

# Start with the Basics

In each childcare center in the town of Reggio Emilia, an *atelierista* guides the projects and work of teachers and children. The atelierista, a trained artist, also uses a knowledge of design to help teachers arrange stunningly beautiful displays that attract the attention of both children and adults.

You do not need to be an atelierista to create beautiful displays that capture both children's and adults' attention. By understanding and using a few principles of art design you can create displays that

◆ present children's work attractively
◆ permit children to reflect on their past experiences
◆ encourage children to talk, discussing and reflecting on the events represented on the display
◆ document and communicate children's work for parents, school personnel, and the community

Learning about and then applying the principles of *color, line, texture,* and *composition* will allow you to create artistic displays.

# Color

Think about the power of color when you select materials for a display. How would you feel, for example, if you were asked to eat a piece of blue chicken? And how flavorful do you think a plate of white food would be? Psychologists know that certain colors are calming and that other colors such as grays, blacks, and browns seem to sadden people. Bright colors attract the eye, while subtle tones and hues are good backgrounds for children's work.

The colors you select to display children's work have the same kind of power. Look at a color wheel. One half of the colors on the wheel are warm (red, orange, and yellow), the other half cool (green, blue, and violet). The warm colors of red, orange, and yellow demand attention and stimulate people. Cool colors have the opposite effect of calming people.

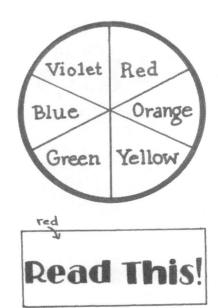

### Warm Colors

Artists use colors from the warm half of the wheel to catch the eye. When you place something red, orange, or yellow in a display, you know that children's eyes will automatically focus on these colors. Use bright red, orange, or yellow in a display to say, "Look here!" This highlights the things you want children and adults to notice.

Or you might use dashes or spots of warm colors on a display to draw people's attention to specific items, such as a large yellow star, bright red sun, or orange petals of a flower. Bright, warm colors might be used for the title or captions on a bulletin board or other display. Or, frame text you want people to read in red or another warm color.

### Cool Colors

Green, blue, and violet are called cool colors, perhaps because they remind us of woods and water, and appear to calm people. This is why cool colors, such as pale greens and blues, are often used in hospital or crisis settings. You can use this principle with children as well. If you want calm children, avoid painting walls in any red tone, and rather than choosing bright red or yellow furniture, select furniture that is natural wood tone or if plastic or painted, in tones of light green, blue, or violet.

Cool tones can be appealing backgrounds for a display. You might use:

◆ pale violet paper to frame a child's scribble or other work.

◆ a light green cloth to cover a tabletop on which to display children's box constructions

◆ blue wallpaper as the background for a bulletin board

pale violet paper

See Our Dances

blue wallpaper

### Primary Colors

Yellow, red, and blue are primary colors. These are primary because they can be mixed to make the secondary colors green, violet, and orange. The primary colors are intense and can assault the eye if used in excess. They can add dash and spice to an exhibit or display, but only when used sparingly.

### Neutral Colors

Neutral colors from nature offer endless possibilities in displays. Neutral colors—white, beige, sand, icy-bluish gray—are lovely and calming. The following examples illustrate how neutral colors can be used effectively:

◆ Tones of white—use different shades and degrees of white, which can range from warm creams to icy blue, to create a background to display children's paintings. One teacher used this type of background effectively to display children's paintings of white swans that they had observed in a nearby park.

Use shades and degrees of white for background.

mount on neutral brown piece of cardboard.

- Weathered wood—use a few weathered boards of neutral beige and brown to form the backdrop for children's wood construction.
- Fallen leaves—paste fallen leaves on a piece of cardboard. During the fall, three-year-olds in Reggio Emilia gathered fallen leaves. With the help of the teacher they pasted the leaves on a piece of cardboard to form a collage. The teacher picked up on the soft brown, golden beige tones of the leaves by mounting the display on another neutral brown piece of cardboard.

## Using Colors

In most displays you'll use a variety of colors. The three major ways of using colors are:

- to use colors from one half of the color wheel, called a harmonious display
- to use shades of the same color, called a monochromatic display
- to contrast warm and cool colors that are opposite each other on the color wheel, a display of complementary colors

By using colors from only one half of the wheel, either the warm or cool colors, you will provide a harmonious display. By using tones and shades of one color, you can create a monochromatic display.

### Harmonious Display

Blue, indigo, and violet and their tints, which are next to each other on the color wheel are harmonious and give a cool sophistication to a display. Warm colors—yellow, orange, and red—are harmonious together as well. These warm colors give a display exuberance and warmth.

### Monochromatic Display

Here are two examples of using monochromatic colors.

- If children have gone outside to observe clouds, you might provide them with a few shades of blue and white paints so they can recreate their experience of observing clouds. These can be displayed on a background of differing shades of blue or white to unite the entire display.
- You can use cloths of different shades of yellow, from the palest to the most brilliant, as a backdrop for children's

drawings and paintings of a field of wild daisies.

### Complementary Colors Display

Using colors that are opposite each other on the color wheel, such as blue and orange, red and green, purple and yellow are called complementary colors. Using colors that are opposite each other or that complement one another provides interesting contrasts and attracts the eye. That's why green and red are so popular at Christmas, orange and green during Halloween, and pale yellows, pinks, blues, and greens during spring.

Look at the color wheel and choose colors that are opposite each other to create attractive displays.

For example:
 ◆ Display children's paintings of sunflowers that are primarily yellow using a blue-toned piece of paper or cloth as a background.

Display on a blue-toned paper or cloth

Pumpkins displayed against a background of light green wallpaper.

- A mural in one of the schools in Reggio Emilia depicts children running through a field of red poppies against a background of green leaves, stems, and fields.
- Display children's paintings of orange pumpkins with green leaves and stems, created after a trip to the pumpkin farm, against a background of light green wallpaper.
- Combine yellow and lavender papers as a background to display children's depictions of spring flowers.

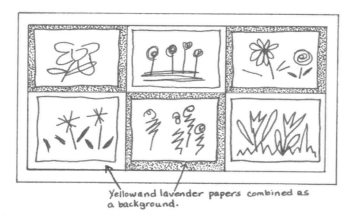

Yellow and lavender papers combined as a background.

## Lines

Lines, like colors, can be used to create attractive displays. Look around at the details in your environment. What lines do you see? Bookshelves often have straight lines dividing books and curved lines at the top that lead the eye to the next shelf. Lamps and shades often consist of round lines, and tiles on the floor form slanted lines.

Some lines seem to continue, like the roundness of the light fixture; others are repeated, such as those formed by the tiles on the floor. Artists use lines to express feelings and ideas.

Use lines to:
- divide spaces
- direct the eye to specific places

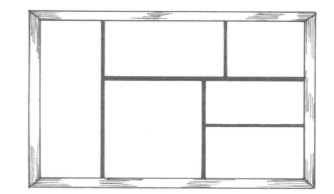

## Dividing Spaces

You might use straight or curved lines to divide spaces on a bulletin board.

## Directing the Eye

Curved lines create rhythm and flow, and they direct the eye throughout the display. You might use curved lines to create a display of framed artwork or other objects. The line could be made of:

◆ twisted crepe paper
◆ a piece of string or ribbon
◆ a ribbon of sparkling stars, Halloween pumpkins, or spider webs
◆ strips of paper

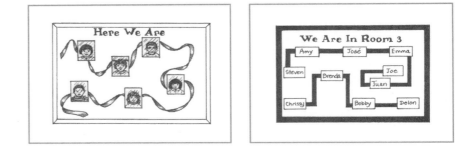

## Diagonal Lines

Diagonal lines mean action. They move the eye in their direction. Use diagonal lines to direct the eye to different parts of a bulletin board or display.

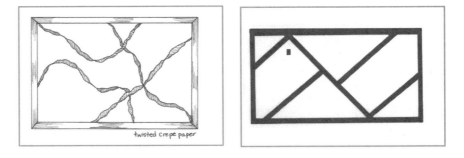

## Straight Lines

Horizontal lines can be used as a baseline or horizon in a display. They add calmness to a bulletin board or display.

 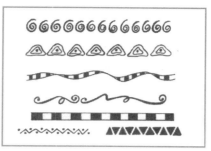

### Using Lines to Decorate

Lines can be used in a display to create patterns or form a design. You might use lines to create a decorative border, or to frame photographs or pictures in a display.

# Texture

Texture in a display produces interest. By using texture you invite the eye and hand to explore, examine, and really look at a display. Touch the textures around you. What feels smooth? Rough? Hard? Sandy?

Like color, using textured materials in displays creates tones or values. Using different textures such as net, mesh, wire, burlap, sandpaper, textured paper, upholstery, chenille, or other fabric, also adds interest in the same way color does.

Use textured areas as backgrounds or backdrops to display simple objects and paintings that are without texture. Examples include:

- ◆ Burlap—display smooth clay products by placing them on a backdrop of burlap. The contrast between the rough burlap and smoothness of the clay is appealing and provides interest to the display.

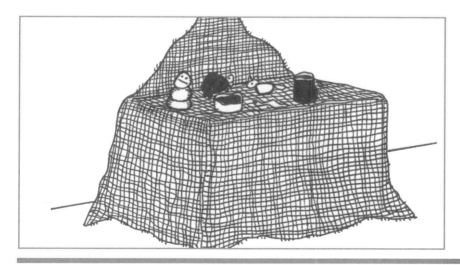

◆ Silk—place photos of the children on a background of watered silk. The pattern of the silk enhances the colors and movement in the photos.

◆ Screening or Sandpaper—display children's drawings of a construction site on large sheets of screening or large sheets or sandpaper.

◆ Cotton—mount paintings of clouds on patches of cotton clouds.

## Composition

The arrangement of items, whether on a bulletin board or tabletop, is an important part of any display.

## Balance

If work is displayed all in a row, it looks stilted and uninviting. The arrangement of all materials should be balanced. The top illustration is an example.

## Asymmetrical

Another interesting way of displaying work is not to use balance but to arrange the work asymmetrically. The middle and bottom illustrations show work that is asymmetrically arranged.

## Focal Points

Before arranging a display, identify exactly what you want the viewers to focus on. What is the point of the display? What are the most important things you want viewers to see? Which parts are less important? What do you want children and/or adults to learn from the display?

## Space

How you use space, the intervals or unoccupied areas and voids between and among objects and positive space, determines to a large extent, its beauty, attractiveness, and usefulness.

## Rhythm

To create eye-pleasing displays, artists use continuity of line, shape, color, and repeated patterns, known as rhythm and movement. They also use repeated patterns found in the art of long ago. The Greeks, inspired by trees, constructed columns around their buildings. Today architects create buildings with repeated geometric shapes to create patterns and rhythm.

Similar forms create rhythm, and dissimilar forms interrupt the flow of the eye. Try to plan similarities in your displays. You could use similar colors throughout a display, or repeat textures, shapes, and lines.

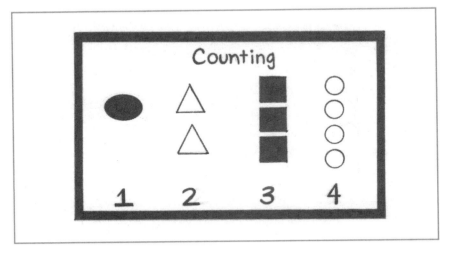

## In Summary

Color, line, texture, and composition are powerful components of a display. How they are used can enhance displays and increase their usefulness. The way things are arranged or composed in a display or bulletin board makes the board or display attractive or unattractive to others.

Warm colors—red, orange, and yellow—are strong and should be used sparingly to attract the eye or highlight a part of the display. Cool colors—greens, blues, and violets—are believed to be calming and are useful to soften a display.

Primary colors are also used to highlight parts of a display, and neutral colors serve as a pleasing backdrop for the important parts of a display. Monochromic displays, all of one color tone, are appealing, as are displays using complementary colors, those opposite each other on the color wheel.

Curved, straight, and diagonal lines are used to divide spaces, direct the eye to specific places, unite a display, or as decoration. Textures add interest to a display. Contrasting one texture against another increases the attractiveness of a display.

# Assessing Your Knowledge of the Basics

To increase your understanding of the basics of art, do the following as you travel, shop, read, or watch television:

◆ Observe how people use color, texture, line, and composition to attract your attention or create a pleasing effect.

◆ In advertisements in newspapers and magazines, note how lines are used to carry the eye, unite the ad, or highlight a part of the ad.

Now look at your displays and bulletin boards.

◆ How are colors being used to attract attention?

◆ Are the warm colors used sparingly, only to highlight special places or items?

Create a monochromatic display of tones of one color or use a harmonious color group. Create another display or bulletin board using complementary colors.

◆ Which display do you find more appealing?

◆ Which display seems to attract the attention of adults and children?

How is texture being used?

◆ Are you using textures in your displays?

◆ Which displays could be enhanced with a piece of netting, burlap, or shiny, smooth foil?

◆ Plan a bulletin board or display around a piece of textured material.

On a tabletop or a large piece of paper, practice arranging different shapes and forms of a variety of colors.

◆ Create symmetrical and asymmetrical compositions. Try adding different lines and textures. Ask your colleagues to judge the attractiveness of each.

◆ Practice with different color groups and combinations, textures, and lines as you continue to create displays or bulletin boards in your room.

◆ Ask an art educator or artists to judge your displays and help you increase their effectiveness by using the basic principles of art.

# Chapter 3

# Framing and Mounting

Do you want to show children you truly recognize and value their work? Then, frame it! It's not necessary to frame or mount each and every piece of art or other work children produce, but framing specific work lets children and their parents know the value and importance of the work.

In addition to demonstrating the value of children's work by treating it with respect, framing and mounting children's work:

◆ helps create appealing displays

◆ showcases specific works

◆ turns children's work into meaningful gifts for family and friends

Teachers who know the *basics of framing*, a variety of ways to *create frames*, how to *display framed work*, and how to *involve children in making frames* have the tools to create beautiful displays of children's work *and* respect the work, as well.

# The Basics of Framing

Frames can be created or constructed from a variety of materials. Among these are:

- colored construction paper
- discarded paper of varying textures, colors, and materials obtained from a local print shop
- pages from a discarded wallpaper book
- paper plates
- unused Styrofoam trays
- box lids
- found objects

The *color*, *texture*, and *size* of the frame can add interest to the drawing or painting or detract from it.

## Color

It's not only the color of the frame that needs to be considered, but also the color of the child's work. The colors you select to frame children's work have the power to create a pleasing, attractive display, or one that fails to capture children's attention.

When framing children's work, find the dominant color in the work you are going to display. Then create the frame or other part of the display using the same color, a different shade of that color, or a complementary color. For example, if the child's painting has an interesting red line wandering through it you might select a shade of red for the frame. Or select a frame that is the same color as parts of the painting but of a lighter or darker shade. A lighter color background or frame can call attention to darker shades of the same color in the painting. Likewise, a darker shade can subdue the same color within a painting. Or choose a very different color from the prominent color in the child's work. Complementary colors are opposite each other on the color wheel; combinations such as red and green, yellow and purple, and orange and blue are complementary. Complementary colors strengthen each other when placed next to one another. For example, you might select a blue frame to complement a child's orange drawing.

## Texture

Texture is not something we actually see, but feel. However, we "see" texture in works of art or their frames by interpreting the patterning of light and dark and color, and we guess what it would feel like.

Frames of differing textures add interest to children's work. For example:

- ◆ Burlap—the roughness of a burlap frame might match or complement a collage of natural objects such as twigs, acorns, seeds, or leaves.
- ◆ Calico—a bright piece of calico or other print could add interest to a drawing or painting of a child's family.
- ◆ Satin or Silk—the smoothness of satin or silk might highlight a painting of flowers.

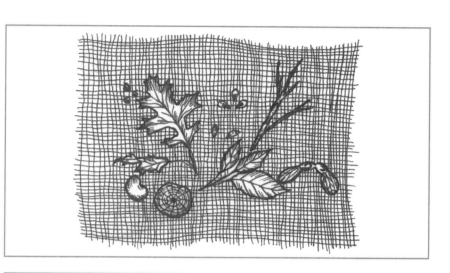

## Size

The size of the frame depends on the nature of children's work. Framing a small 3" x 5" piece in a 12" x 18" frame gives the piece power. Typical frames for 8½" x 11" works would be an inch or two wide. Larger paintings, such as those on easel paper, require wider frames. Professional framers find that making the bottom margin of the frame wider than the sides is more appealing to the eye. The top and side margins should be of equal width, but narrower than the bottom margin.

Make bottom margin of the frame wider than the sides.

You can frame:
- ◆ drawings
- ◆ paintings
- ◆ sewing work
- ◆ weaving work
- ◆ paper collages
- ◆ paper sculptures
- ◆ writing samples
- ◆ reports

## Making Frames

### Simple Construction Paper Frames

Select a piece of colored construction paper that matches or complements the colors in the child's drawing or painting. Use a small amount of library paste on each corner of the back of the painting. Paste the painting on the piece of construction paper, leaving a wider margin at the bottom and equal margins at the top and sides.

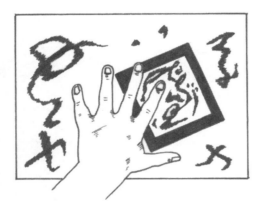

### Framing Parts of Paintings

To highlight younger children's scribbles you could, from time to time, cut a painting or drawing apart in order to better display it.

Select scribbles that hold no meaning to two- or three-year-olds, or those they have discarded. To select parts from a painting that are appealing, make a frame by cutting a rectangle from a piece of white construction paper. Place this frame over areas of the painting. When you see parts that seem to stand out, cut them out and mount them on a contrasting piece of construction paper.

Use the back of the frame to describe children's progress in scribbling. You might write about the control the child exhibited in repeating the circles or dots in the scribble, or how the child used lines throughout the painting. These can make fine gifts to present to parents on special occasions.

### Strip Frames

Measure the painting you want to frame. Cut 2" strips of colored construction or other paper. Cut the length of three pieces 2" longer than the painting and as wide as you wish the frame to be. The fourth piece should be ½" wider than the other three. This piece will be used as the bottom of the frame. Paste strips onto the sides of the painting to form a frame.

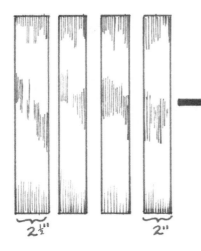

### Two-Color Frames

Use two colors of construction paper to create a unique frame. Cut the first piece of colored construction paper as described in the strip frame above. Cut each strip in the second color wider and longer. Paste the smaller strips onto the sides of the painting. Then paste the larger strips onto the smaller strips.

### Framing a Series

Sometimes children will draw or paint a sequence of pictures. They may illustrate the beginning, middle, and end of a favorite folk tale, such as the Three Little Pigs, or may just draw or paint a series of flowers, animals, or designs. You can mount or frame these as a series. Be sure to include a description of what the children were doing, saying, and thinking about as they drew or painted the pictures. Another idea for series art is to have children paint or draw on a long piece of paper. When they finish creating, fold it accordion-style and display it on a tabletop.

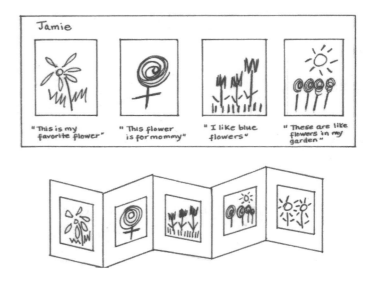

## Wallpaper Frames

Wallpaper adds texture and interest when it is used to frame pictures or paintings. Ask home decorating stores for old sample books or ask parents to bring in leftover wallpaper rolls from their home-improvement projects. Use wallpaper as a background for finished artwork, as a picture frame, or to cover a box to be used as a frame.

## Cut-Out Frames

You don't want to do this very often because children do not need to see any more patterns or stereotypic outlines than they already do. Using patterns of any kind can negate children's creativity. If children are asked to follow an adult's idea of what something looks like, they will begin to doubt their own abilities to draw and create. Doubting their own abilities, children will then ask you to do it for them, or withdraw from drawing and creating all together. But from time to time, perhaps on a special holiday, children and parents enjoy seeing paintings in a special frame. You could cut out a heart, circle, or other figure from a piece of construction paper to create a fancy frame.

## Three-Dimensional Frames

### Triangle Frames

Fold a piece of construction paper, tagboard, or other heavy paper into thirds to create a triangular frame. Cut a frame from the middle third of the paper.

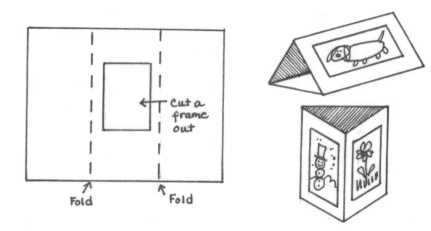

### Box Lid Frames

All kinds and shapes of box lids make fine frames. Think about using clear plastic box lids and the boxes themselves to hold or frame children's three-dimensional collages. Use wallpaper or fabric to cover the books and lids to be used as frames. Some box lids can even be painted before they are transformed into frames. These make special gifts for parents.

## Round Frames

Some of children's work can be displayed in a round frame. For example, drawings or paintings of children playing outside, walking in the rain, waiting for their turn on the slide, or scenes from a Halloween night are suited to mounting or framing in the round.

When children have drawn a scene that could be displayed in the round, simply roll the painting or drawing to form a round and staple the ends together. Or, take a plain piece of 12" x 18" paper, staple the ends together, and paste children's pictures on the round surface.

## Slipcover Frames

Slipcover frames can be used again and again to display special works. Or, a child's work can be framed in the slipcover and sent home as a special gift. To make the frame fold, cut out an opening for the artwork, and staple a piece of tagboard or other strong paper so that paintings of the same size can be slipped in and out.

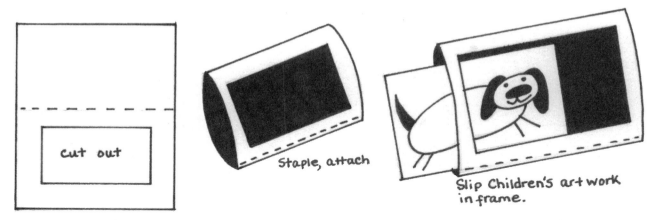

cut out

Staple, attach

Slip Children's art work in frame.

## Pinch Frames

Pinch frames are easy to make. Once you get the hang of making pinch frames, you can show children who are over the age of three how to make them as well.

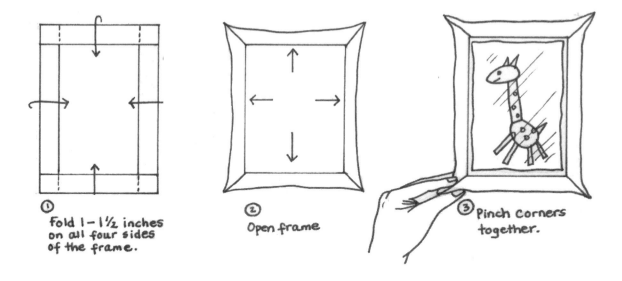

① Fold 1–1½ inches on all four sides of the frame.

② Open frame

③ Pinch corners together.

# Displaying Framed Works

Now that children's work is framed, think about how you will display it.

Artwork should be displayed asymmetrically. If children's work is displayed in uniform rows, it can look stilted and uninviting. The arrangement of framed work should be balanced, but it will be much more interesting if it is not symmetrical. Here are some examples:

Display the children's work in a way that unites the display. Use the principles of line, rhythm, or repetition to unite a display of children's works. You might do this by selecting one color, texture, or shape that is repeated throughout the display. Here is an example:

Or you could use pieces of string or ribbon, a string of stars, Halloween "spider webs," strips of paper, or other items to unite the display.

# Involving Children in Making Frames

With all this framing going on, you'll need a cupboard, a shelf, or a box to keep framing materials together. It doesn't have to be a large place or contain a lot of materials. But keeping rulers, strips of cardboard, fancy papers, wallpapers, different types of cardboard, staples, rubber cement, and other types of glue in one area devoted to making frames may be helpful.

Children should be invited to use the area as well. At first children might work with adults in selecting papers for a frame to highlight a specific part of their painting. An aide, older child, or parent volunteer could help children develop the skills of creating a variety of frames for their work. Once children get the idea of making frames, they can create frames independently.

## Frames Children Can Make

### Natural Objects
Provide children with precut cardboard frames. Children can glue found nature objects—shells, acorns, leaves, twigs, even small stones—to the frame, which can then frame a picture or painting of their experiences.

Leaves          acorn tops          Shells

### Collage Frames
Offer children a variety of collage materials to glue to precut frames. Include paper doilies, buttons and beads that are too large to swallow, colorful papers, stickers, or dried flowers and leaves.

Stones

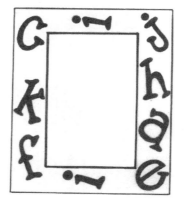

### Thematic Frames

Create other interesting frames to reflect the theme children are or have been studying. Provide precut cardboard frames and precut pictures from magazines representing a specific theme. If the children are studying animals, make collage frames of animal pictures. Children over three could do the cutting and pasting on a precut frame.

### Stamped Frames

Using precut cardboard frames, children three and older can make a design using rubber stamps. Chose stamps that represent a theme or the children's interests.

### Letter Frames

Along with the precut frames, give children an assortment of alphabet stickers. They can make their name with the stickers, or just decorate the frame with letters of the alphabet.

Be sure to label the back of the frame with pertinent information. You'll want to write the child's name, age, and a note about the importance of the framed work.

## In Summary

Children feel valued and respected when their work is framed. Not every piece of work needs to be framed, but from time to time each child needs to see his or her work in a frame. By framing children's work you are:

- ◆ taking the first step in creating appealing displays
- ◆ showcasing specific works
- ◆ turning children's work into meaningful gifts for family and friends

There are a variety of frames you can create—from simple construction paper frames and pinch frames, to more elaborate three-dimensional frames.

Children, too, can participate in framing their own work. Having supplies ready for children's use, demonstrating how to construct a frame, or having cut frames ready for children to decorate enables them to become involved in framing. By doing so children gain respect for their work, themselves, and help to beautify their environment.

# Assessing Your Frames and Displays

Over a period of time, ask:

◆ Do I frame the work of all children?

Are framed displays changed to reflect:

◆ current themes and projects?
◆ the interest of children and others in the school?
◆ current events?

Are framed displays:

◆ titled?
◆ described with their meaning, what the children were thinking of, representing, or doing when they created the work?

To involve children in displaying their work do you:

◆ ask children to participate in selecting which of their work to display and in constructing the display?
◆ keep blank paper strips, stick-on letters, and stick pins on hand so children can create their own displays?

# Chapter 4
# Tops—
# Tables, Shelves, Windowsills and Ledges, and Boxes

Much of children's work is not suitable for framing. After all, children construct realistic and fanciful objects from boxes and found objects; they fold and join paper to construct a house, school, or other environment; and model three-dimensional objects from clay or dough.

Yet, it's important that children's thematic or project work be displayed. Displaying ongoing work stimulates children to extend their ideas and expand the theme. Displays of a completed project or unit help children recall the past and foster their thinking about past events.

That's where tops come in. *Tabletops, standing shelves and the tops of shelves, ledges and windowsills,* and *sturdy boxes* can be arranged in ways to display children's:

- ◆ three-dimensional constructions
- ◆ clay work and sculptures
- ◆ booklets, books, and reports
- ◆ textiles they have woven, hooked, or sewed
- ◆ social studies thematic and project work
- ◆ science projects
- ◆ mathematical conclusions
- ◆ musical adventures

◆ masks
◆ materials reflecting their cultural heritage

Anything three-dimensional that is interesting and meaningful to children can be displayed. Initially, the idea to display something—a piece of art or thematic and project work—will come from the teacher. Once children are involved in arranging the display, choosing items to display, and dictating or writing titles and explanations for the display, they will initiate ideas for displaying their own and group work.

Find ways to make tops appealing places to display children's work. You can cover a cardboard box, hollow block, or small table with:
◆ an attractive cloth
◆ a discarded tablecloth
◆ netting of any color or type
◆ brightly colored tissue paper
◆ a piece of rough burlap

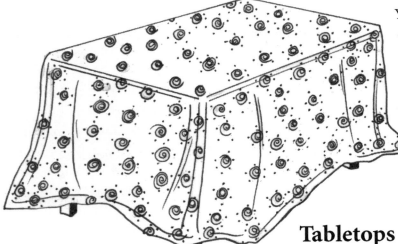

You might find scrap material at a fabric or upholstery shop. Take an empty box labeled with your name and phone number to a store. Ask the manager to fill it with the scraps they otherwise would toss out and then call you when the box is filled. This is a great way to pick up lovely pieces of velvet, silks, and other textured, colorful fabrics.

# Tabletops

Be on the lookout for small, discarded tables that could support displays of children's work. The school's storeroom is the first place to look. Continue to look for small tables at flea markets or garage sales, or ask parents to donate small tables suitable for display.

Tables that aren't particularly pleasing to the eye can be covered attractively, or combined with bulletin boards, pieces of cardboard boxes, or cardboard frames.

TOPS—TABLES, SHELVES, WINDOWSILLS AND LEDGES, AND BOXES

## Standing Shelves and Tops of Shelves

Regular classroom shelves make fine display cases. The top shelf can hold a triangular frame with the title and a narrative about the display, and perhaps a book or two on the topic. Children's work would be displayed on the shelves.

Some displays can be contained in clear containers on the shelves. Children may have collected seashells, acorns, and leaves; or sorted plastic cars, animals by type or color, or some other category. Shelves are perfect for displaying these collections.

Two shelves placed back to back offer a larger top for displaying objects, and more shelf space for displaying objects and viewing them.

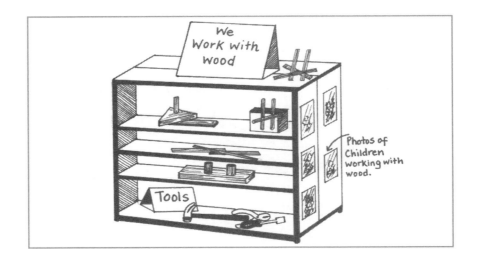

Math materials can be displayed on two shelves back to back. The top can hold a variety of materials such as shells, buttons, nuts and bolts, acorns, and pinecones for weighing, measuring, counting, and sorting. The bottom shelves can hold work cards illustrating or describing what task children could complete with the materials.

A shelf, serving as a divider, offers additional display spaces. Paintings, drawings, and other paper work can be mounted on the back of the shelf, with three-dimensional items placed on the shelves.

## Windowsills and Ledges

Think of using windowsills, ledges, or hanging shelves as places to display children's three-dimensional projects and other work.

## Windowsills

You're lucky if you have windowsills where children can display objects that catch the light or where you can grow things.

Use the windowsill to display:

◆ **Paintings** created on discarded plastic lids, inside plastic cups, or inside clear plastic boxes. Collect a variety of plastic objects, such as clear lids from cookie or candy boxes, clear plastic boxes, of blank overhead sheets. Add a bit of detergent to regular easel paints and have children decorate or paint pictures inside the clear plastic containers. Display on a windowsill to capture the light.

◆ **Stabiles** made of light-catching materials. Stabiles are the opposite of mobiles. Instead of hanging down like a mobile, stabiles stand up. To construct stabiles you'll need a solid base. You can use wet clay, solid, plastic packing Styrofoam, or pieces of rolled cardboard. Give children pipe cleaners or

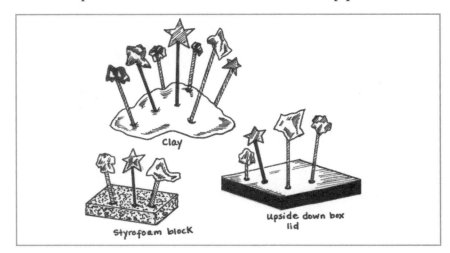

Clay

Styrofoam block

upside down box lid

some sort of sturdy wires (discarded telephone wires are good) to hold the decorations. Children can attach clear, shiny, cellophane papers; bits of aluminum foil; stars; and other decorative materials to the wires. Then, position the wires in the base.

◆ **Seeds** planted in clear plastic cups. Cover the cup with black paper, and then plant the seeds. After the seeds sprout and grow, uncover the cup to view the roots.

## Ledges

Displaying things on ledges is an effective way to use wall space three-dimensionally. Attach a fancy border to a plain wooden shelf and mount this ledge on the wall at children's eye level. Use ledges to display:

◆ photos of the children at home or school

◆ special art objects for looking, not touching, that children bring to school or that belong to you

◆ clay objects or ornaments constructed by the children

◆ special books that children already know and love or those you want them to get to know

◆ special collections

In one class, children collected a variety of acorns from different types of oak trees and displayed these on the ledge. In another class, children used a ledge to display shell collections, and in another, children displayed a variety of beautiful stones and rocks they found in their own backyards.

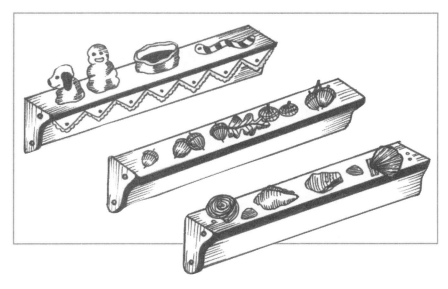

# Boxes

There's no better resource than an empty box! They're wonderful for displays.

## Refrigerator Box

Get a large packing box or an actual refrigerator box. If necessary, cut the box so it is about as tall as the children. Help the children

paint the box white. Then ask them to look at the front of a refrigerator (in their kitchen or the one at school)and paint a door handle, hinges, and other things on the front of one side of the box. This will be the class refrigerator.

Place a tape dispenser on the top of the "refrigerator" and if appropriate, a box of tacks. Put something heavy in the bottom of the box, perhaps a couple of heavy books or blocks, for ballast so the box won't tip over.

Children then use all four sides of the "refrigerator" to post a note to someone, or put up a reminder, or to display their favorite painting. Many children find this a better place than a cubby to keep a painting or picture before taking it home.

### Sturdy Cardboard or Wooden Boxes

Ask your local supermarket to save sturdy packing boxes or wooden crates for you. These can be stacked in a number of ways to provide places to display children's work.

Two Boxes

Three Boxes

Four Boxes

## Triangular Spaces from Boxes

Obtain large cardboard boxes. Cut off the tops, bottoms, and one side of the box. Open it up like the illustration:

Choose a cool or neutral color water-soluble wall paint to paint the triangle  These can be placed on the floor, a tabletop, or shelf to display children's work or photos of children at work.

# Involving Children in Creating Displays

### Tabletop Dioramas

Tabletops can be used to make and display dioramas, miniature scenes reproduced in three dimensions. Creating and playing with dioramas help children to develop mapping skills, reflect on an experience, and express their ideas. When building a diorama, children recreate their ideas and images of an experience, even a vicarious one. As they reflect, draw, and build, they gain ideas of space, location, and perspective.

### Firsthand Experiences

To create a diorama children first need to have an experience to recreate. A field trip to a fire station, nearby mall, or a longer trip to a farm, zoo, or airport is required. Before the trip, draw a map of the route you will take. Include drawings of the center or school and other familiar landmarks. Show children the map and consult it as you walk.

Children can work together in small groups or as individuals to create a diorama. After the diorama is finished, the children enjoy playing with it, acting out different themes, and taking on different roles. Even after the diorama seems finished, children will continue to add details, make changes, and rearrange the scene.

Title the dioramas and use a triangle frame to display photographs of children on their field trip and a few descriptive sentences about the trip to inform others.

Depending on the children's experiences, you could create a variety of dioramas. For example:

◆ **Walk Through the Neighborhood**—After a stroll through the neighborhood, children could build a diorama of the houses, buildings, parks, and other things they've observed. Cover the top of the table with a piece of brown wrapping paper or a discarded sheet. On the paper or sheet, draw a central street and a few landmarks.

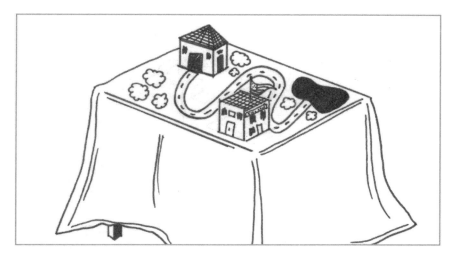

Give children a variety of empty paper boxes, small milk cartons, assorted papers to cover the boxes, paste, tape, staplers (with adult supervision), and other materials needed to build with paper boxes. Have a container of markers so children can draw more streets and add other details. Provide small plastic people, cars, trees, or other miniatures for children to use.

◆ **Trip to a Farm**—After a trip to a farm, the children could build a barn, farmhouse, pond, and barnyard. Help the children begin by drawing a footprint for the house, and then draw a path from the house to a footprint of the barn. Put a box of blocks on the table for building the barn, house, and other buildings, and provide plastic or wooden farm animals and other farm equipment. (See illustration on the next page.)

◆ **An Airport**—To recreate an airport, cover the table with a white sheet, draw a place for the terminal and a few runways. With boxes, small airport-related toys, and markers, children can create an airport. (See illustration on the next page.)

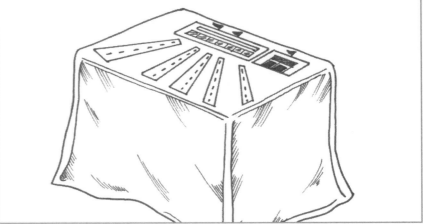

Build other dioramas following a trip to:

- ◆ the apple orchard to pick apples
- ◆ a local mall
- ◆ a fast food restaurant

### Vicarious Experiences

Familiar stories and poems offer vicarious experiences that can be expressed through dioramas. After children have become familiar with a story, you and they could recreate the story on a tabletop. You'll want to have the book available for children to consult as they build and play with the diorama. Some examples are:

- ◆ **Wynken, Blynken, and Nod**—Once children are familiar with the poem, *Wynken, Blynken and Nod,* you can create a tabletop diorama of their trip "across a river of crystal light and into a sea of dew." Cover the tabletop with a piece of blue fabric, bunching it up to simulate waves. Provide silvery materials so children can make the moon and stars, boxes to make the wooden shoe boat for Wynken, Blynken, and Nod, and netting so children can make nets. Shiny paper, fabrics, or other materials should be available to make fish. You can use small dolls to represent Wynken, Blynken, and Nod, or children could construct these figures from fabric and other scraps.

◆ **In the Tall, Tall Grass**—A walk through tall grass or to a small pond, followed by reading Denise Fleming's *In the Tall, Tall Grass* or *In the Small, Small, Pond*, could lead to the construction of a diorama of life in the grass or pond. If you want to recreate grass, you could cover a table with Easter basket grass. Provide small plastic animals for children to hide and then find in the tall grass. Cover a table with blue cloth so children can recreate the world of a small pond.

Box with plastic and wooden insects and animals.

◆ **Where the Wild Things Are**—Children love Maurice Sendak's *Where the Wild Things Are.* Cover a table with brown paper and draw a pathway on the paper. Add a couple of plastic trees and paint a blue pond. Ask children to make their own "wild things" using construction paper and markers.

# In Summary

Tabletops are great places to display children's three-dimensional work, art objects, collections, or other items. A tabletop by itself may be rather uninviting, but tabletops covered with attractive cloth, pieces of burlap, or pieces of tissue paper invite children to look, touch, and explore.

Combining a tabletop display with bulletin boards or cardboard displays enhances the usefulness of the display. Photographs, labels, or two-dimensional artwork can supplement and complement the display.

If you don't have room to display objects and children's work on tabletops you could use classroom shelves, ledges, or windowsills to display light-catching objects, books, or any other object.

Sturdy wooden or cardboard boxes are great for displays, as well. These can be stacked, arranged in groups, or in rows to display children's work.

Children can participate in creating their own displays. Providing children with a theme, a few objects, and plenty of art supplies enables them to create their own tabletop dioramas.

## Assessing Tabletops and Other Displays

Ask yourself:

- ◆ How visible are the displays?
- ◆ Are they at the children's eye level?
- ◆ Can adults use the displays as well?
- ◆ Can children and adults handle the displays?
- ◆ Are the displays kept organized, cleaned, and ordered?
- ◆ How often are the displays changed?
- ◆ Are children involved in creating the displays?
- ◆ Do the displays actively involve children?
- ◆ Are there materials, pieces of cloth, and small objects for the children to use to create dioramas and other displays?
- ◆ How often do children interact with a display with adults or other children?
- ◆ Do children ask to build dioramas?
- ◆ Do adults in the school and/or children's parents stop to talk about the display?

# Chapter 5

# Interactive Bulletin Boards

Bulletin boards are a staple of the early childhood classroom. They should be important focal points that are full of meaning. The bulletin boards and murals that children create should be physically close to them. Mounted at children's eye level, the children can see and feel them, talk about what they see and feel, and reflect on their experiences.

Bulletin boards and murals are also meaningful to children because they extend from the children's experiences and expand on them. They are integral parts of the curriculum because today's boards stem from the children's daily experiences in their classrooms, not from the administration or teacher.

Bulletin boards and murals:
- ◆ document children's work and communicate with others
- ◆ give children the opportunity to reflect on their experiences
- ◆ decorate the room
- ◆ involve children in creative work

**Document Children's Work and Communicate with Others—**
Some bulletin boards and murals are arranged with the specific purpose of informing others in the school, children's parents, and members of the community about the nature of developmentally

appropriate practices in early childhood and how and what young children learn in the preschool/primary classroom.

**Give Children the Opportunity to Reflect on Their Experiences—** Bulletin boards and murals give children the opportunity to extend and expand on their experiences and discuss their work with others. Some boards are designed to engage children. A number of boards are designed to engage children in arranging the board or some other activity.

**Decorate the Room—**Even though the major purposes of bulletin boards are to increase communication and extend the curriculum, they also serve to beautify the room and school. Use boards that are too high for children to become involved with to create points of beauty in the room.

**Involve Children in Creative Work—**Children benefit from creating their own bulletin boards. When children work together arranging a board or a mural, they learn the give and take of cooperation, gain communication skills, and feel like a part of the group.

This chapter describes how to create attractive boards that provide a means of communicating, reflecting, and expanding children's work; decorate the room; and involve children in creating boards and interacting with the boards.

## Creating Attractive Boards

Today's boards are designed to be attractive to both children and adults. Backgrounds, textures, borders, and principles of design help to beautify the environment and affirm children and their work as they communicate to others.

### Backgrounds

Backgrounds are secondary in bulletin boards. This doesn't mean, however, that the background is unimportant. Backgrounds support, complement, and enhance the content of the board. But when backgrounds are not carefully chosen, they can also detract from the board, lessening the board's usefulness and attractiveness.

Select material for the background with color and texture that supports the work to be displayed on the board. Choose soft, neutral shades and hues of colors and simple, subtle designs for the background. If the color is too strong, too bright, or too warm, or if the design is too bold, it will disrupt the display.

Primary colors probably should not be chosen for backgrounds. An orange construction paper background jumps out at the viewer, hiding the message of the items on the board.

As with framing, consider the dominant colors of the materials you want to display. Then select a background color that either complements these colors, or matches them to form a monochromatic display.

Texture can add interest to a board. Subtle fabrics and textured papers can create a backdrop for the display. Materials that make attractive backgrounds or can be used on other parts of the board include:

◆ netting
◆ burlap
◆ wallpaper odds and ends
◆ calico
◆ silk
◆ velvet or other fabrics
◆ upholstery fabrics
◆ foil and other shiny paper

## Borders

Borders help keep children's and adult's attention focused on material displayed on the board. When thoughtfully arranged, however, bulletin boards do not require a border. Rather than making a stilted, stereotypic border of cutouts, paper fringe, or other material, incorporate the border as a part of the board. For example, one teacher made tall trees and placed these at the sides

of a board about children's study of wood. The trees served the purpose of decorating the board while preventing the eye from wandering.

When the class created a board about their study of butterflies, the teacher used some of the butterflies the children had made as a border.

After a study of spiders, the teacher made a board "All About Spiders." She used Halloween spider webbing to create a border.

A board about plants growing around the center and immediate neighborhood was bordered with pieces of trailing wild grape vines.

A board titled "Starry Nights" was bordered with wires of stars.

During a study of wood, another teacher created a board called "All About Woodworking". She used burlap for the background and bordered it with pieces of unfinished wood dowels.

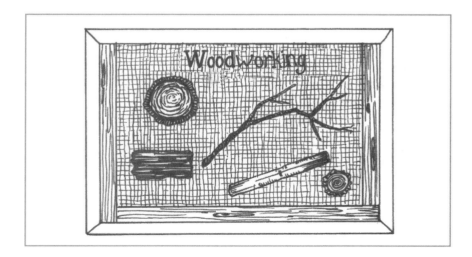

### Design

Less is more when it comes to designing bulletin boards. A crowded board is unattractive and fails to communicate anything to anyone. Instead of crowding a board, select:

◆ a goal for the board
◆ a few photographs or pieces of children's work
◆ a design for the board

**Goal**—What message do you want the board to give? What is the purpose of the board? The answer to these questions will help you select photographs, children's work, narratives for the display, and the title.

**Photographs or Pieces of Children's Work**—While it is important to display the work of every child in the group over time, you do not need to put every child's work on the same board. Keep an informal record of children's work that has been displayed, or is being displayed elsewhere in the room or center.

**Design**—You might pick a monochromatic color scheme and an asymmetrical design. Before placing items on the board, arrange them on a piece of paper or on the background you're going to use. After arranging the items you want to display, take a few steps back and look at the display from a distance. Rearrange items until you're satisfied with the design.

Use the basics of display (see Chapter 2) to arrange items on the board in symmetrical or asymmetrical ways. Experiment using shapes and forms in the composition.

## Documenting and Communicating with Others

Bulletin boards document children's work and communicate to others how and what children are learning while in the early childhood program. These boards can include a combination of photographs of children at work, their artwork or other representations of their experiences, as well as factual information about the topic. Access to a camera, preferably a digital camera, will be necessary in creating these boards. Topics for these boards that document and communicate are drawn from every content area and for every purpose.

Two effective bulletin board topics include "Getting to Know You" and "Getting to Know Others."

**Getting to Know You**—When children and their families first join a classroom, you'll want to help them become acquainted with each other and the school. Begin by creating a board titled "Our Friends." Read *Making Friends* by Fred Rogers (1996) and *Do You Want to Be My Friend?* (1988) by Eric Carle. Then take a photo of each child and as you do so, interview him or her. Ask him or her to tell what a friend is or what he or she thinks about friends.

Attach copies of children's photos to the board. Label each with the child's name. Above each child's head, draw a bubble, similar to a comic strip bubble, and write what they said about their friends.

Because the photos of the children are the focal point of this board, use a neutral background and a black or other dark-colored marker to label the board.

**Getting to Know Others**—Help children become familiar with others in the school and their roles. Arrange for children to meet teachers and aides in other groups, the school's janitor, director, secretary, cook, bus driver, and other workers in the school. Take photos of these people at work and children interacting with them.

Attach photos of the workers and children to the board. Label them with their names. Write a few sentences describing the role of each worker.

# Reflecting, Expanding, and Extending Children's Work

Bulletin boards can be used as a way to summarize or conclude a theme children have experienced. These boards, which stem from every content area, permit children to reflect on past experiences, and some can even serve to extend and expand on these experiences.

To do so, however, children need to have actual experiences that can be represented on a board.

## Social Studies

Topics from social studies can be extended through bulletin boards. Boards stemming from children's study of geography, history, and economics can be created. These can include photographs of the children as well as selected drawings, paintings, and other artwork. Examples of how to expand and extend learning in geography and history follow.

### Geography

A concept key to geography is that we live on the earth. Humans change the earth they live on, travel on and above the earth, and experience the effects of the rotation of the earth around the sun.

**Travel**—The concept that people travel on the earth can be introduced to very young children by studying how they travel. A board titled "How We Come to School" could summarize this study.

Ask children to list the ways they travel to school. They may walk or ride in a car, bus, or van. Offer children a variety of papers, markers, scissors, and paints to represent the car or bus they use to get to the center. Cut these out and mount them on a road you've drawn on a bulletin board.

You can expand the study of travel by taking field trips to a local subway, train or bus station, or airport. After the trip, construct another board.

**Mapping Your Travels**—As you travel around your neighborhood, consult maps. You could use a picture map of the area or draw your own map. As you walk or travel, show children where they are on the map.

Back in the classroom, make a map of the route you took on the trip. Place photographs on the map to depict important landmarks children saw along the way. Draw trees, streetlights, and other landmarks as well. Highlight the school and the place you visited with stars.

Children can contribute to the map by cutting out things they saw along the way or at the place they visited. Photographs of the children as they traveled enhance the board.

**Ideas Travel**—Ideas travel, too. How people get information to one another is a part of the study of geography. Bulletin boards can help children expand their study of how ideas travel.

Younger children might study how the mail is delivered. For them, the bulletin board would include photographs of their class visit to the post office, as well as photos of children writing letters to one another and receiving mail at their classroom mailbox. In addition to paper, markers, and envelopes, give children junk mail stamps to use to mail their "letters."

Make a bulletin board of children's addresses and phone numbers. These can be displayed under a picture children have drawn of their home, or a photograph of themselves or their home. Emails sent and received can form the basis of other boards (For safety reasons, displays with names and addresses should always be located in a classroom, never in hallways or public spaces of the school.)

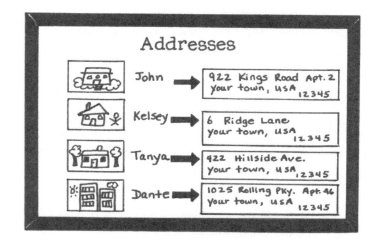

**Change**—No matter where you live, someone somewhere is in the process of moving and changing the earth. Whether you live in New York City; Santa Fe, New Mexico; or Earlville, Maryland; you'll be able to find a construction site for children to observe.

Take photographs of children observing the work at the construction site. After returning from the trip, provide children with an array of papers cut into rectangles, circles, squares, and triangles; 12" x 8" paper; and paste. Choose colors that reflect the equipment that children observed. Mount children's creations along with the photographs, titling the board "Construction."

## History

Just because young children have a limited sense of time or the ability to remember the past does not mean the study of history is not for them. Young children enjoy and benefit from the study of their own immediate past.

**We Grow**—Start with a bulletin board that charts children's growth. Read A. A. Milne's poem "The End" found in *Now We are Six* (1927). The poem begins by describing what it was like to be one year old, then two, three, four, and so on. After reading the poem have children illustrate what they were like when they were only one and just begun, when they were two and nearly new, three, and so on.

**Growing Board**—Continue the study of growth and aging. Ask parents to send a baby photograph of their child and a current photo. Or you can take a current photo of the child. Frame the photos with strips of paper or mount them on interesting pieces of wallpaper or other construction paper. Place the baby photos above the photos of the children. Title the board, "We Are Growing Up."

**Aging Board**—Everyone ages. Construct another board to illustrate the fact of growth and aging. Ask teachers, administrators, and other school personnel to bring a photo of themselves as a child and a current photo. This time title the board, "Guess, Guess? Do You Know Who the Baby Is?"

After mounting the photos, place the baby pictures and current pictures randomly on the board. Give each photo a number. At the bottom of the board, in a covered folder, place the numbers of the photos that go together.

**History of the School**—Just as children and people change over time, so does the school. Create a "history of our school" board, charting the changes that occur over the year in the child care center or school.

**Our Tree**—Observe a nearby tree as it changes during the seasons. Have children sketch or paint the tree at different times of the year. Label the drawings with the date or season.

## Science

Topics from life, physical, and earth sciences provide content for bulletin boards. Children's study of the plant and animal life around them can be extended through bulletin boards. Likewise, as children explore the physical sciences through toys and everyday events, their experiences can be reflected on boards.

### Life Sciences

One group of children collected chrysalises of Monarch butterflies. The teacher took photographs of them in the field collecting a few of the chrysalises to take back to the room. The teacher photographed the children observing the chrysalises, and then she took another series of photographs when the butterflies began to emerge.

Children used paints, paper, and markers in a variety of orange, ochre, brown, and black colors to match the colors of the butterflies. The board, titled, "All the Beautiful Butterflies," was constructed by first covering the board with a piece of pale salmon-colored netting, which provided texture. The photographs were mounted on a darker shade of orange. Children's collages, paintings, and drawings were then arranged asymmetrically on the board.

### Physical Science

Children's toys can offer the opportunity to introduce children to concepts from the physical sciences. Ask children to observe the toys they play with and start to think of those that move. Ask how they move. Do the toys need someone to move them—for example, dolls, blocks, or toy cars? Or do the toys have an energy source? What is it? Which toys move because you wind up a spring? Which because they have batteries? Others may move because of a wound rubber band.

After the children have examined and played with a number of toys, taking them apart to find out why they move and experimenting with making them move, you can create a bulletin board that categorizes the toys by their energy source.

| People | Rubber Bands | Springs | Batteries or Electricity |
|---|---|---|---|
|  |  |  |  |

Children can draw pictures of toys or cut out pictures from magazines or toy catalogs and attach these to the board under the correct category. This promotes reflection on their previous experiments with toys and helps them extend and expand on their ideas.

# Decorate the Room

But, you may say, the bulletin boards in my center are all high on the walls. Way too high for any child to even see, much less learn from them. What can I do? Boards that are too high for children's use are those that can fill the room with beauty. However, these do need to be changed several times a year to keep the room fresh and up to date.

First, decide on a theme for boards too high for children to view. Nature offers an abundance of beautiful things to arrange on boards. Works of art offer other opportunities to beautify the room, as do a variety of multi-colored and textured fabrics and papers.

### Nature
Cover the boards with cloth or papers of soft and neutral colors. Then create designs on the boards from:
- seashells
- fall leaves
- branches and vines

### Art
Cover the boards with soft and neutral-colored materials to display:
- prints of famous paintings
- photographs of children working/playing
- paintings of children

### Fabrics and Paper
Create pleasing boards using fabric and paper, including:
- soft colored netting draped over the boards. You might add fabric butterflies, bees, or flowers to the netting
- sheets of tissue paper covering the boards. The dark colors will show through the lighter colors.
- scraps of fabric from a local upholstery shop. Drape them over the boards or simply cover the boards with a variety of fabrics.

# Involving Children in Making Bulletin Boards and Creating Murals

Bulletin boards can be arranged to promote children's involvement. These could be in the form of learning stations, flannel boards with things for children to move around, or murals.

### Learning Stations

Some bulletin boards can serve as learning stations where children can practice or gain a skill, or just play with the things on the board. Some examples are:

**Write-On Boards**—Start by selecting a topic that is of interest to the children. Then cover a child-height bulletin board with brown mural paper or other heavy paper. Ask the children to draw their ideas on the board during play or work time, or any other time they have a thought to share about the topic. A plastic or paper box, or a basket can be attached to the board to hold the markers.

Some topics of interest might stem from a favorite story or poem:

◆ After reading *Harold and the Purple Crayon* by Crockett Johnson, put purple markers in the box and tell children this is the place for them to use purple crayons, just as Harold did.

◆ Read *It Looked Like Spilt Milk* by Charles G. Shaw and after you've gone outside and looked at the clouds, children can draw their own "spilt milk stories" on the write-on board.

◆ After reading Christina Rossetti's *What Is Pink?: A Poem About Colors,* fill the basket with pink and red markers and have children draw/write their ideas about pink.

◆ Use it as a message board to draw, write, and scribble an idea about a book or any other topic.

◆ Attach a piece of colorful yarn or heavy string over a chalkboard or cork bulletin board. (See illustration on the left.)

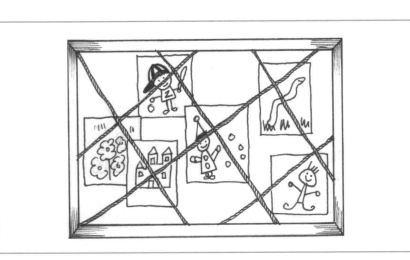

Then children can arrange their own paintings, notes, drawings, or even objects on the board by placing them under the string and removing them as they wish.

## Flannel Boards

Cover the board with a piece of flannel or other fuzzy material. Then, based on the goals of your program, provide children with flannel or Velcro-backed pictures to place on the board. Examples are:

Attach a piece of velcro to back of pictures.

◆ Story Sequence: Cut apart discarded, used picture books. Attach a piece of flannel or Velcro to the backs of the pictures. Place in an attached basket for children to put on the board to tell the story.

◆ Recalling a Sequence: Take photographs of the children shopping for materials for an aquarium, arranging the plants, and adding snails and fish. Put small pieces of flannel or Velcro in the corner of each photo and place them in a basket. Children can show how they set up their aquarium. Or, take photographs of children planning, digging, and planting a garden and have children arrange these in sequence.

◆ Grapheme Awareness: Title the board, "Make Your Name." In one basket, place cut-out letters with Velcro backing. In another, put name cards so children have a model of how to make their name or someone else's name.

◆ Number Practice: Make several circles of yarn on the board. Provide a basket of cut-out Velcro-backed numerals and another basket of cut-out pictures of toys, animals, dinosaurs, butterflies, or other things. Children choose a number and place it inside one of the yarn circles. Then they place the number of objects corresponding with the number they chose.

## Murals

Creating murals gives children an opportunity to organize what they've learned and reach conclusions. Participating in a group art activity, however, is not easy for young, egocentric children. Murals require children to share their artwork with the works of others. This is a difficult thing for young children to do and requires some practice.

Begin by dividing a large sheet of mural paper into sections. Make sure you have at least one section for each child.

Now children can choose where to work, and what media they will work with, to fill their own space by:

◆ creating a wild thing for a board titled "The Wild Things" after they are familiar with Maurice Sendak's *Where the Wild Things Are.*

◆ drawing, painting, or constructing a picture of what Little Miss Muffet did after she was frightened away by the spider.

◆ expressing their idea of a field trip, what they saw or what impressed them after a trip to a store, the fire station, or post office.

◆ painting or drawing their friends.

When it's time to change the board, you can cut it apart and each child can take home his or her own painting.

Another idea is to divide the mural into halves. Give children sponges and a dish of blue paint to paint the sky on one half. When the sky is dry, give them a bowl of green paint to paint the grass on the other half.

Then children can use the board to:

- draw and cut out animals that live in the sky or on the earth
- things they see in the sky and on the earth
- vehicles that transport people through the air and on the earth

With these two divisions the group could create holiday murals.

- For Halloween, each child could draw, paint, or use other media to create a picture of themselves on Halloween night. This time the sky would be dark, however. Title the board, "On Halloween Night." Or they could make a pumpkin to paste on a board titled, "At the Pumpkin Farm."
- At Thanksgiving, each child could contribute a painting on the mural of something they are thankful for.
- For Valentine's Day, the children could paint a picture of love in their space on the mural.
- Children could paint a tree or other plant on the baseline of a mural created to celebrate Earth Day or Arbor Day.
- On Japanese Kite Day, children could draw themselves flying a kite after they've done so on the playground.

## In Summary

Bulletin boards add a great deal to an early childhood setting. They serve to document children's work, communicate with others, give children the opportunity to reflect on their past experiences (extending and expanding them as they recall their immediate past), decorate the room, and involve children in meaningfully creating their own boards.

Attractive bulletin boards are created using the basic principles of display. The background is carefully chosen so it does not detract from the message of the board. Areas of the board that are important are highlighted with primary or warm colors. Rather than detracting from the board, borders are integral to the board.

Children will become involved in first-hand experiences with bulletin boards. Some can be constructed as learning stations and flannel boards, while children will help create others in the form of murals.

## Assessing Bulletin Boards

Ask yourself:

◆ Are the bulletin boards in my room and school attractive to children and adults alike?

◆ What basics of design have I followed to ensure their attractiveness?

◆ How do I know children are involved with the boards? Which children stop to look at the boards, handle the things on the boards, or talk with others about them?

◆ Is each child's work or photograph found on the bulletin boards throughout the room and school?

◆ Are the boards changed frequently so children have an opportunity to reflect on current work?

◆ How do I know if adults gain meaning from the boards? Do adults look at the boards? Talk about them? Ask their children or teachers about them?

# Chapter 6

# Graphing, Surveys, and Other Data

Young children are scientists. They research and explore their world to discover more about the earth and their immediate environment. Like scientists everywhere and in every field, young children use the scientific processes of observing, questioning, collecting data, organizing information, and reaching conclusions.

**Observing**—Children look, listen, feel, and take apart to learn more about their world.

**Questioning**—Scientists begin their research by asking a question. Young children are full of questions. Two-year-olds ask, "What's this? What's that?" Three-year-olds ask, "Why? Why? Why is the sky blue? Why?" Fours want to know, "How does this work? What does this do?" And fives continue questioning, asking, "What would happen if?" "What comes next?" "When will I be big?"

**Collecting data**—Using their immediate surroundings to relate to the world, young children, like scientists, collect information about their world. They count, categorize, and gather information as they observe and question.

**Organizing information**—Through the use of graphs, surveys, and charts young children, just as scientists do, begin the process of organizing their information.

**Reaching conclusions**—Finally, children will reach conclusions about the information they've gained through their observations, questioning, collecting, and organizing.

Throughout the scientific process, children can be introduced to the multiple ways of displaying records of their observations and questions, and displaying and organizing collected data. Children can display their work and conclusions through:

◆ graphs
◆ surveys
◆ collections that categorize their findings
◆ murals that summarize their ideas

Whichever form you choose to display children's beginning thinking skills, you will need to involve the children. Even though you will often be the one to initiate the activity, plan ways of involving the children. The more fully children are involved and engaged, the more meaning the graph, survey, or categorizing activity will have for them.

Graphing, conducting surveys, categorizing information, or making murals gives children a way to answer a question or solve a problem. Through these methodologies, children have a reason to observe, a way to organize their observations, gain information from them, and reach conclusions. Because young children are not able to understand the abstractness of the methods, each begins with concrete objects.

When a child asks a question to another, "I have a dog—he's my pet. Do you have a dog?" Or poses a problem, "I don't want to make vanilla pudding—I like chocolate," or "I need a red marker—all the red markers are gone. Red is my favorite color," you have an opportunity to introduce graphing, surveys, categorization, or making a mural.

# Graphs

### Block Graphs

All kinds of things can be graphed with blocks. Children can use block graphs to find out interesting information about their classmates and the world around them.

**About Favorite Colors**—Label a chart with the sample colors and children's names. Each child places one block under his or her favorite color. Count the blocks to find out how many children like each color and which color is the overall favorite.

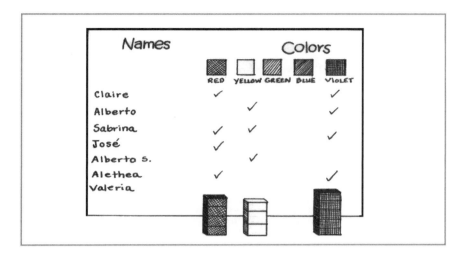

**How Many Pets?**—To find out how many children have pets in their homes, make a chart of type of pet (e.g., cats, dogs, fish, birds, insects, reptiles, and include a space for No Pets) and the children's names. Each child places a block under the appropriate category. Count how many children have pets and do not have pets and find out what kind of pet is the most prevalent.

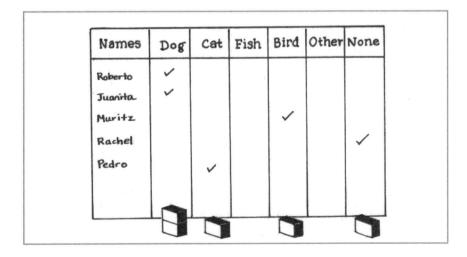

| Names | Dog | Cat | Fish | Bird | Other | None |
|-------|-----|-----|------|------|-------|------|
| Roberto | ✓ | | | | | |
| Juanita | ✓ | | | | | |
| Muritz | | | | ✓ | | |
| Rachel | | | | | | ✓ |
| Pedro | | ✓ | | | | |

**Brothers and Sisters**—Do the same to find out how many children in the group have siblings. Label a chart Sisters, Brothers, and None. Children can create a graph using blocks. Count the number of children who have siblings, those who do not, and how many siblings are boys or girls.

**What Do You Want to Learn?**—At the beginning of the school year one teacher asked children to tell what they wanted to learn during the year.

| Name | What We Want To Learn | | | | |
|------|------|-------|---------|---------|---------------|
| | Read | Write | Numbers | Science | Our World |
| Kyle | | ✓ | | ✓ | ✓ |
| Kerri | ✓ | | | ✓ | |
| June | ✓ | ✓ | | | |
| Jeanna | | | | | ✓ |
| Tim | | ✓ | | | |
| mitch | ✓ | | ✓ | | ✓ |
| Kim | | | ✓ | | |

**What Kind of Shoes?**—What kind of shoes are you wearing? How do they stay on your feet? Do they have buckles, shoestrings, Velcro, or are they slip-ons? Find out which is the most popular style of shoe in your group by graphing shoe types with blocks.

## Object Graphs

Once children are used to making graphs of blocks, you can make graphs using any other object. The objects could be toothpicks, Legos, paper squares, or symbols to represent their ideas. One class used empty and washed milk cartons to make a graph of how much milk they drank on a given day of the week.

You could use:
- birthday candles to determine which month has the most birthdays.
- stickers of stop signs to indicate which foods children do NOT want to eat.
- seed pods collected from gum, maple, oak, or other trees during the spring or fall to represent trees.
- paper squares to represent homes to graph how many children live in apartments, single-family homes, duplexes, trailers, and so on.

◆ toothpicks to measure how many times children can hop on one foot. Paste them on a chart called, "I Can Hop."

## Line Graphs

Cash register tape can be used to make graphs that measure things. In the process of using the tape, children are introduced to the idea of measuring things and the importance of being able to organize their observations and reach conclusions.

**How Tall?**— Using a piece of cash register tape, measure the height of each child. On the piece of tape, record the child's name and height. Paste each tape on a chart labeled "We are Tall." Rather than pasting the strips from tallest to shortest, paste them randomly so children are challenged to find their tape and talk about height with each other.

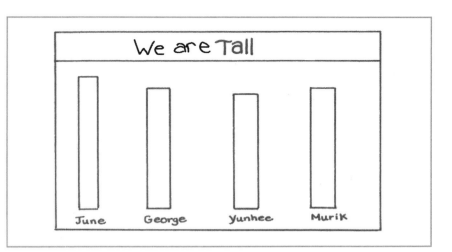

**How Tall Are the Flowers?**— Make a garden and involve children in planting seeds that germinate and grow quickly, such as scarlet runner beans, sunflowers, or morning glories. Then, with cash register tape, measure how tall the flowers are when they first sprout, as they start to grow, and when they're fully developed. Measuring the growth of the flowers helps keep children interested in watching their garden grow. Pasting the tapes on a chart helps them reflect on their experiences.

**How Far Can You Jump?**—Use tape to measure other things as well. After children have seen an Olympic event or other sports event, show them how to broad jump. Then, using the cash register tape, measure how far each child jumps. Paste the tapes to a chart labeled

"Our Broad Jump." However, avoid making this activity into a competition. It's fun just to see how far you jumped.

**How Long?**—Continue measuring activities by finding the longest, tallest, or widest piece of equipment on the playground using cash register tape. You'll need children to cooperate and work together to do so. Together they can measure the swing set, jungle gym, slide, and other equipment. Be sure to label the tape and record how high the pieces of equipment are. Back in the classroom paste the tapes on a chart, and add photos or drawings of the equipment. If children are interested in measuring, they can continue measuring things in the room and their center.

## Pictorial Graphs

**Who Am I?**—A favorite graph, one that is teacher made, is a pictorial chart of children's eye and hair color. Have children look in a mirror and tell what color their hair and eyes are. Then they pick the color most like their hair and eyes from an assortment of eyes and hair you have precut for them. Children paste their choice under their name on the chart.

| Name | Eyes | Hair |
|------|------|------|
| Sally | 👁 | 〰 |
| Bryan | 👁 | 〰 |
| Kathy | 👁 | 〰 |
| Keith | 👁 | 〰 |
| Allan | 👁 | 〰 |

**How Many?**— A group of children watching a spider climb their classroom wall began counting the number of legs on insects they found on the playground and in their room. They soon discovered that spiders have eight legs, but insects have only six. They made a picture graph of the insect and arachnids they found.

Then they began counting insects' eyes, wings, spots, and feelers and graphed these with pictures.

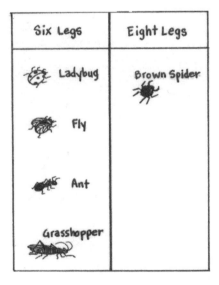

| Six Legs | Eight Legs |
|----------|------------|
| Ladybug | Brown Spider |
| Fly | |
| Ant | |
| Grasshopper | |

|  | Eyes | Legs | Wings | Feelers |
|--|------|------|-------|---------|
| Grasshopper | 2 | 6 | 2 | 2 |
| Ant | 2 | 6 | 2 | 2 |
| Spider | 2 | 8 | | |
| Ladybug | 2 | 6 | 2 | 2 |

Once children get the idea of counting things and recording their findings in pictorial graph form, you can make other graphs:

◆ How many wheels are on a fire truck, delivery truck, and the teacher's car? How many horns are on each? How many seats? How many steering wheels?

| HOW MANY WHEELS? | |
| --- | --- |
| Fire Truck | 12 |
| Car | 4 |
| Delivery Truck | 4 |
| Oil Truck | 16 |

◆ How many children like strawberry, chocolate, or vanilla ice cream?

| Who Likes Ice Cream? | | |
| --- | --- | --- |
| Strawberry | Vanilla | Chocolate |
| Ming Yi | Misha | Rosa |
| Boris | Vanessa | Casey |
| | | Bryan |

◆ How many different types of buildings are around the neighborhood? Count how many single-family homes, apartment buildings, and office buildings you find when walking around the block.

◆ How many people work in the center? Go on a walking trip through the school to find out how many people work there and what they do. Take Polaroid photos if you can.

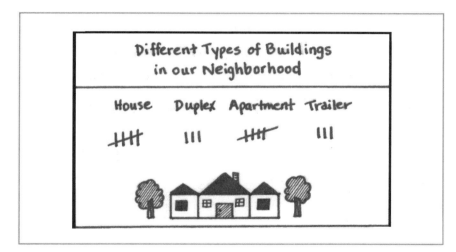

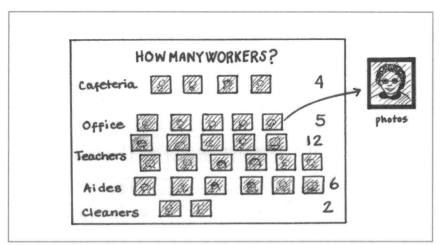

## Surveys

Give children clipboards and markers, and they'll make up their own surveys. For two- and three-year-olds these surveys will take the form of role-playing, with children taking notes as if they were doctors and nurses, clerks, or their parents.

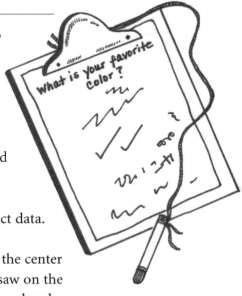

Children as young as three years old can use clipboards and markers to keep track of and organize data that can be mounted and displayed. Four- and five-year-olds will use clipboards in more directed ways as they observe and collect data.

**Why Is There Trash on the Sidewalk?**—On a walk around the center a group of four-year-olds were upset about the trash they saw on the sidewalk. They took great pride in keeping their classroom ordered and clean, and they asked, "Why do people do that? Don't they know it's garbage?"

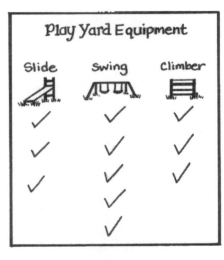

The teacher suggested they ask people in the neighborhood that question. Together the children and teacher designed a survey form. Children, with the teacher's help, stopped people walking by the center and asked them the questions on their survey. Some people said, "Maybe the people who threw trash really didn't think about it," and "There's no trash can around." The children's next mission was to save money to buy trashcans for the front of their center.

**What Do We Want?**—One school's PTA gave a class of three-year-old children money for new equipment for their playground. The teacher used this as an opportunity for children to study their playground, and make a list of the equipment they had. The teacher then provided several copies of a catalog of outdoor equipment appropriate for three-year-olds. These were placed on the library table with the directions to read through the catalogs and mark on a graph the equipment they wanted. After children read through the catalogs and discussed the choices with their friends, the teacher took duplicate catalogs and cut out pictures of the equipment that seemed to be most appealing to children. She made the following chart and then each child marked his or her choice. The class used the money to buy the equipment that received the most marks.

**Our Favorite Games**—With clipboard in hand, a child asked a visitor to the four-year-old group this question: "Do you like 'Duck, Duck, Goose;' 'Doggie, Doggie Where's Your Bone;' or 'London Bridge'?" When told "Duck, Duck, Goose" was the favorite, she made a check mark on her survey next to the picture of a duck.

**What Do We Like?**—Surveys can be taken to examine children's likes and dislikes as a group. Once children get in the habit of taking surveys, they can informally collect information about others' likes and dislikes on their own, such as a survey about "What Story Do You Like the Best?" One way to make it easy for children to survey their friends is to create a master copy of a survey by placing a photograph of each child down the left side of the page. Make copies and place them on clipboards for the children to use as they wish. Children can make tally marks next to the appropriate faces for any given survey.

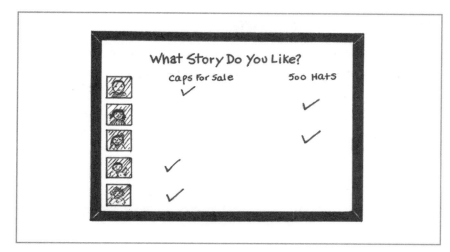

# Categorizing

Children's natural need to find out about and order the world in which they live leads them to categorizing things in their world. Displays can include charts, scrapbooks, and other everyday objects. And don't forget all of the things children can categorize while they're playing outside.

Set the stage for categorizing by:

◆ Asking children to place new equipment in the appropriate center. For example, if you bring in a new book ask children where the book belongs in the room. Do the same with a new piece of housekeeping equipment, a board game, math game, musical instrument, and so on.

◆ Making scrapbooks. Staple a few pages of paper between two sheets of construction paper and place the blank books in the writing area so children can use them as they wish. Every now and then, set up a table for making specific scrapbooks. As young children cannot handle magazines and cut out pictures at the same time, provide them with a bunch of pre-cut pictures of animals, flowers, or whatever else you want children to categorize in their scrapbooks. They can make scrapbooks about:

  ◆ Animals That Live in the Zoo (sorting zoo animals from precut pictures of farm, domestic and other animals)
  ◆ Birds I See (choosing birds they have seen from a bunch of pictures of birds)
  ◆ Clothes I Wear
  ◆ Toys I Would Like
  ◆ Cars I Like

◆ Making Charts. Charts can categorize information, as well. One teacher cut out pictures from magazines and labeled a wall chart "Red Things". Children cut out red things and pasted them on the chart. They continued with other color charts.

Another teacher had children use cutouts or draw their own pictures, making charts of:

- ◆ Rain clothes
- ◆ Party clothes
- ◆ Summer clothes
- ◆ Clothes we never wear

## Categorizing Things

Tabletop displays can be made of children's categorization activities. Provide children with objects and things to sort and have a variety of sorting boxes handy. You might make a sorting tray by gluing plastic glasses to a piece of plywood or even a heavy sheet of cardboard.

Or you could glue clear plastic boxes to the board.

Find clear plastic boxes and create dividers for these with pieces of plastic or heavy cardboard.

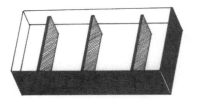

Flannel boards can be used as well. You could use pieces of yarn to divide the board or other pieces of flannel.

Then provide children with collections of:

- seashells
- nuts and bolts
- buttons (make sure they are too large to be inserted in noses or other places)
- bells—cow, decorative, sleigh, or other bells
- fabric, wallpaper, or tile squares to sort
- large marbles of all types to play with and sort by color or type
- plastic animals to categorize by farm, zoo, pet, or wild
- old greeting cards to play with and sort

### Categorizing Outdoors

As children play outdoors, they naturally sort and categorize rocks, seeds, flowers, soil, and other objects found on the playground or around the school. Provide children with clear plastic bags or clear plastic boxes. They can start collections in these, or put all the smooth round rocks in one box, the soft, limestone in another, and so on.

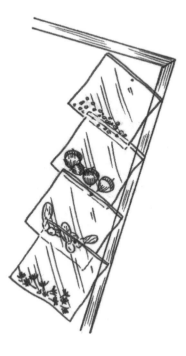

In one class, children collected fall seeds in plastic baggies. The teacher made a display of the bags.

# In Summary

Children need a way to organize their thoughts and ideas. By introducing them to graphing, conducting surveys, categorizing, or summarizing their ideas in murals, children are being introduced to the basics of thinking. When children have questions, graphing and conducting surveys help them to collect and organize data and find answers to their questions.

To do so, however, requires that after the graphing or other activity is completed, teachers guide children in the use of the graph, chart, or survey. You can ask children to determine which is the longest, what is the favorite color of the class, how many children have pets and so on. Or ask them what the graph or chart shows or means to them.

When designing the graphs or surveys, remember some of the basics of design. Use neutral colors for the background, and warm colors to highlight information on the chart or graph. Consider whether you want your graph to be monochromatic or colorful. Use lines to direct the eye and divide spaces, as well as to present information. When possible, introduce different textures into graphs and surveys, either as background or as part of the graph itself. Finally, consider balance, symmetry, focal points, space, and rhythm.

## Assessing Graphing, Surveys, and Categorizing

The first thing you need to assess is how involved were the children in the activity:

◆ Did the purpose stem from the children themselves? From a child's question? A class problem?

◆ How were the children involved in making the graph or chart? What parts of the graph did they make?

◆ How appealing and meaningful were the graphs or other forms of recording data to the children after they were made? Did children consult them? Talk about them together?

Then you'll want to ask yourself how meaningful the graphs or other charting methodologies were to the adults in the school.

◆ How many parents stopped to look at the graph?

◆ Which talked about the graph with their children?

◆ How many mentioned graphing to you?

*Chapter* **7 Islands of Beauty**

The places where children learn should be as beautiful as the children themselves. Each and every room can be a place of pure, simple, elegant beauty. A beautiful environment informs children how to behave and interact with others. Surrounded by beauty, children are motivated to create beauty themselves. Everywhere children look, they should see an island of beauty. Islands of beauty can consist of:

- a clean, ordered environment
- growing things
- natural things
- hanging things
- works of art

**A Clean, Ordered Environment**—Most schools do not have the luxury of a classroom and building designed just for children, yet all, regardless of the nature of the physical setting, can plan and arrange for children to be in an uncluttered, clean, and ordered environment. This means that each room children occupy, including the bathrooms and places where they eat and nap, are clean, ordered, full of beauty, and communicate to children that they are valued.

**Growing Things**—Green plants and flowers, fish in well-equipped aquariums, insects and animals living and growing in well-constructed terrariums beautify a room.

**Natural Things**—The beauty of nature, seashells, leaves, twigs, acorns, seeds, rocks, and stones, beautify children's world.

**Hanging Things**—Mobiles have been used to beautify public places for centuries. Mobiles designed to catch and reflect light, move as the air moves through them, display current projects, or fill the air with pleasant sounds can be a part of the preschool classroom environment.

**Works of Art**—In addition to displaying children's work, teachers can introduce children to the artwork of others. Throughout the room and school, display artwork from a variety of artists and illustrators.

# A Clean, Ordered Environment

## Cleanliness

Obviously, children's environments must be clean and safe. In good schools for young children:

- tables, chairs, and other furniture are washed daily.
- floors are swept throughout the day and washed after children leave the center.
- toys and other equipment are checked daily. Broken equipment and toys with parts missing are removed, as is equipment with sharp edges or parts that are loose and could be swallowed or stuffed in some orifice.
- everything is disinfected daily by washing with detergent in water, rinsing with clear water, wiping with a solution of two tablespoons chlorine bleach and one gallon of water, and sun or air dried.

## Order

Cleanliness is not enough, however. Everything in classrooms should be ordered. Instead of clutter, children should see choices. Rather than putting out every piece of equipment or toy possible, carefully select a few pieces of equipment, toys, or objects for each center. The practice of selecting a few objects or items for children to choose does a couple of things. Doing so forces you to change learning materials on a continual basis, so you are more likely to continue to meet children's changing needs for challenge and stimulation.

When a few materials are displayed you can more easily respond to children's changing interests. You can easily add items, perhaps books about insects or model insects, when children are pursuing "bugs" in their world. Or you can readily remove items when children lose interest, perhaps replacing them with items that follow a new interest or stimulate children to learn something new.

By selecting and displaying a few things at a time you:
◆ help children see the possibilities of each material
◆ enable children to see the materials and reach them by themselves
◆ help children categorize their world
◆ give children an opportunity to keep their own things in order

**Help children see the possibilities of each material.** For example, scissors, stored point down in an upside down egg crate, are displayed along with a box of scrap papers and glue sticks, suggesting their use.

Upside down egg crate.

**Enable children to see the material and reach it by themselves.** Cluttered shelves clutter children's minds, and they become unable to see individual objects and make choices. Clutter also prohibits them from reaching exactly what they need or want without knocking other materials or objects off the shelf.

**Help children categorize their world.** Display materials in clear, plastic boxes by category. For instance, things to use in a collage may be stored in separate, clear boxes—feathers in one box, beads in another, and wood pieces in still another box. Materials used to join things together, such as staplers, hole punches and brads, and an assortment of paper clips, could be kept in the same box. Another box might contain an assortment of glue, and still another would hold pieces of ribbon or fabric scraps.

**Give children an opportunity to keep their own things in order.** Order gives children the opportunity to participate in returning items to the right shelf and keeping their own things in order.

Order continues in the elegant way teachers display children's artwork. Just as shelves are not cluttered with everything, neither are the walls of the classrooms completely covered with children's work or other things. Displaying everything all of the time negates the purpose of displaying children's work. When walls are filled with work, children have no way to focus on a display and reflect on their past experiences or extend their current work. The clutter distracts their eyes and their brains become overloaded with things to think about, so they turn away, avoiding the cacophony they see on the walls.

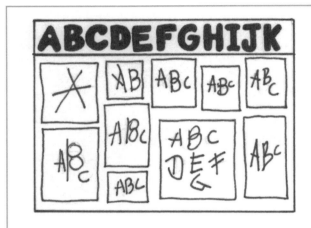 

# Growing Things

### Plants

Green plants that only need a bit of sunlight and little care are the least expensive way to beautify a room. Green, growing plants beautify the children's bathrooms, their sleeping and eating rooms, and of course the rooms in which they work and play.

One teacher placed the cubbies at the back of the room in a U shape. She arranged a number of potted plants on the tops of the cubbies, forming the wall toward the room. These plants beautified an otherwise awkward space in the room.

Each area of a classroom can have its own special plants that add beauty. In the south, gardenias and other plants are easy to grow inside and out. The west has cacti and other succulents. Find the plants in your region that are hardy and demand little care for the amount of beauty they add to your environment. Tried-and-true plant possibilities include:

◆ sweet potatoes
◆ philodendrons
◆ primroses
◆ African violets

**Sweet potatoes.** Look at the potato and find an end with "eyes." Prop the potato in a container of water so the "eyes" are covered with water. Within a few days you'll see the potato beginning to sprout and before long, you'll have a lovely vine to drape over the piano, on a shelf or windowsill, or hang in the bathroom. In addition to catching some rays, sweet potatoes need an occasional change of water. Or you could begin sprouting them in a container of soil, keeping the soil moist.

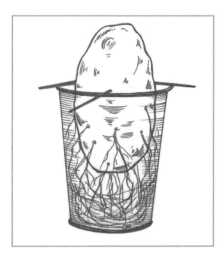

If you plant the potato in a clear, plastic container or vase, be sure children notice the roots as they begin to grow from the bottom of the potato, and ask them to predict what will grow from the top.

**Philodendron.** These plants are poisonous when eaten so they must be hung high, out of reach of the children. They are inexpensive and readily available at any plant nursery. Or if you don't want to buy one, ask a friend for a sprig or two or three of one of their philodendrons. You can turn the sprig into a plant by planting it in moist soil. Keep the soil moist until the sprigs root, then water occasionally.

**Primroses.** Bring in primroses when they first appear in the spring. They're relatively inexpensive. They do need daily watering; however, their bright, cheerful colors will add beauty to any room. When they droop or lose their flowers, enjoy the greenery. When you tire of them inside, take them outside and have a planting party. Plant in partial shade, not full sun, and they'll bloom again.

**African violets** add brightness to the room as well. They are inexpensive and easy to grow. Keep a few plants in strategic places, on the library table, in the housekeeping area, on the piano, shelf, or file cabinet. With a number of plants, sunlight, and plant food, you're sure to have blossoms nearly all year round.

### Involve Children

Involve the children in planting the seeds of the scarlet runner bean in a discarded container. Add a couple of dowels for the plants to climb as they grow. Keep in the sun and watch how fast you'll have a growing and blooming plant for children's bathrooms or other rooms. An added bonus—you can eat the beans produced by the scarlet runner!

cut tops of root vegetables.

Cut the tops off of carrots and other root vegetables such as turnips, rutabaga, or celery. Involve the children in planting just the tops in a shallow container of soil. First cover the bottom of the container with small stones or Styrofoam peanuts for drainage. Have the children plant the tops of vegetables in the soil until only the very top of the vegetable is visible. Then watch them grow into lacy, green room decorations. Plant the tops of turnips, beets, onions, and parsnips together in a shallow pot.

## Living Things

Living things add islands of beauty to the room, as well. Aquariums, though sometimes tricky to balance and keep healthy, add beauty and calmness to the room. Terrariums, clay pots, coconut shells, pinecones, and logs all provide places for beauty to flourish.

### Aquariums

Flat-sided fish bowls and aquariums are best, but require a cover so fish will not jump out. A cover also limits water evaporation. Purchase a pump and guppies, goldfish, or other inexpensive fish. You do not need a lot; a few will do. A snail or two will help keep the tank clean. Consult an aquarium shop on the care of the aquarium. Children should not be involved in cleaning the tank because of the possibility of the spread of disease from snails and fish, but they can help feed the fish.

## Terrariums

Terrariums are true islands of beauty in any classroom. These should be built and managed by teachers because of the issues of health and safety, yet children can take some responsibility for finding food for animals living in the terrarium.

To build a terrarium, obtain a large, glass container. An old leaky aquarium, or a fish bowl, or even a wide-mouthed glass jar can do very well as a terrarium. Cover the bottom of the terrarium with sand and gravel for drainage, and then add leaf mold mixed with soil. This will aid aeration and drainage. Mix some more soil with a little crushed charcoal and cover the previous layers. Bank this last layer slightly toward the back and the sides of the terrarium. Choose small plants and mosses native to your area. Taller plants should be planted deeply, and mosses can be laid on top of the soil. Add rocks and twigs for interest. If you want, push a shallow dish into the soil, place rocks around the rim, and fill with water for a pond.

Now you'll have a place for children to keep insects they've captured and other small animals such as snails, toads, or frogs. Catch flies for food.

## Outside a Window

Not all beauty is inside the room. Make a couple of bird feeders to mount outside a classroom window to attract the beauty birds bring to our environment. A bird feeder can be made from a:

- ◆ clay flowerpot
- ◆ coconut shell
- ◆ log
- ◆ pinecone

**Clay flowerpot.** Place material in the hole of the bottom of the pot, twist a coat hanger around the pot and fill with birdseed. Hang from a limb of a tree or hook near the window.

**Coconut shell.** Saw the end off a coconut shell and twist a coat hanger around it. Hang from a tree limb or a hook near the window.

**Log.** Drill holes about 3" in diameter in a 12"-18" log. Pack holes with suet or a mixture of suet and peanut butter. Drill a hook into one end of the log and hang.

**Pinecone.** Stuff pinecones with a mixture of seeds and peanut butter and hang outside the window.

# Natural Things

Wherever you live, nature surrounds you. Bring as much of the beauty of your natural environment into the classroom. Some things you bring in will not only beautify your room, but foster children's learning as well.

### Rocks and stones

Display beautiful rocks you find in your driveways or yards. Rocks differ in texture, density, weight, color, and luster. Arrange a variety of smooth river rocks in a basket for children to handle and rearrange, or collect a variety of sand stones, stones with fossils embedded, or stones from other areas, such as a variety of gemstones.

### Seeds and Seed Pods

Seeds and seed pods have beauty of their own. A basket of different sizes and kinds of acorns can be displayed simply for beauty of for children to handle and sort into piles. A basket filled with all types and sizes of pinecones appeals to children as well. Other seed pods, such as chestnuts, black walnuts, and other nuts are beautiful in and of themselves.

### Gourds

Gourds and pumpkins beautify a room in the fall. These could be displayed on a tabletop or in a basket.

### Twigs

Look at the shape and form of vines and branches. Clip a few that are exceptionally beautiful and display in a vase. Put a few rocks in the bottom of the vase for stability. Cut some branches from fruit or other blooming trees, forsythia, or azaleas and place in a vase of water. You'll be rewarded with blossoms in a few days.

## Blooming Things

While you do not want to pick every wild flower or cultivated flower you see, from time to time, you can pick and display a few wild flowers that grow in your area. A few thistles, Goldenrod, Queen Anne's Lace, trumpet vines, cow vetch, or Black-Eyed Susans can beautify the room without destroying the ecosystem. If you plant zinnias, daisies, purple cone flowers, Black-Eyed Susans, or other flowering plants unique to your area, you'll have plenty of blossoms to decorate the room from spring through fall.

## Shells

If you're lucky to live near an ocean or waterway, you'll have plenty of shells to display. If not, you can purchase shells from a science shop or borrow shells from someone's collection. The beauty of the shells appeal to children. Display a variety on velvety cloths or in clear plastic, yet beautiful bowls. The display could lead to a study of what lived in the shells and where the creatures lived before the shells were found on the beach.

## Vegetables

Think of the beauty of a deep purple eggplant, the velvet red and green of bell peppers, and the interesting nooks and crannies of a head of cauliflower. From time to time, create a decorative display of vegetables to brighten a room. Then, after the display has been enjoyed, you can wash the vegetables, cook them, and eat them.

## Other Things

Wonder with children about the colors in a moth or butterfly's wings. Go outside to look at a rainbow and wonder out loud about where the ends of the rainbow are. Look at the symmetry found in the weeds growing in sidewalk cracks, and glory in the beauty of a bud just beginning to open.

## Involve Children

Involve children in arranging the displays. They may find rocks for the display, or arrange shells in ways that appeal to them. Ask them to sketch the blooming branches or other natural things you've carefully arranged to create islands of beauty.

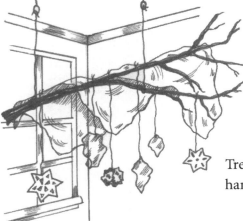

# Hanging Things

Taking your cue from mobiles, hang things from the tops of windows or the ceiling to add other types of islands of beauty in your room.

### Limbs

Tree limbs downed in a storm? Find one of manageable size and hang it from the ceiling. But not before you decorate the limb with:

- bits of mirrors to catch and bounce back streams of light
- cut different shapes from pieces of heavy cellophane to refract light
- cut snowflake-like shapes from white tissue paper or shiny aluminum paper
- drapes of gauzy netting in soft, pleasing colors
- dried leaves, acorns, or other attractive seed pods found in your area

### Mobiles

Create mobiles from simple coat hangers. As with the tree limbs, hang bits of mirrors or other light-catching materials at different levels.

Or create a theme mobile. One teacher put two coat hangers together and created a "Mitten Mobile" for winter. It looked like the illlustration to the left.

### Clotheslines

No place to display children's work? Stretch a rope or old clothesline across the room from one wall to another. If you want it out of reach of children and for adults only, hang it higher on the wall. If

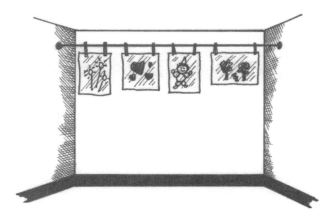

not, string the rope at children's eye level. Then you can clip paintings, drawings, or even objects to the line as you and the children wish.

### Wind Chimes

Fill the air with pleasant sounds by adding a wind chime to your room. You can purchase any wind chime or create one yourself. Make wind chimes from a piece of wood with drilled holes and:

- ◆ discarded silverware
- ◆ bamboo
- ◆ clay pots

**Discarded silverware.** Securely attach discarded forks, spoons, or other silverware to a round piece of wood with drilled holes. Hang the silverware at different heights for a pleasing effect, but make sure the objects will touch each other in a breeze.

**Bamboo.** Cut a bamboo pole into 6"-12" lengths. Drill holes in one side of the cut length. Thread and tie string through the holes and attach to a piece of wood.

**Clay pots.** First, find a small piece of wood or other object, perhaps a discarded pencil stub, one for each pot. Tie a piece of heavy string in the middle of the stub and insert one into the hole of each of the small clay pots. Because of the weight of the pots, you'll need a sturdy base on which to attach the pots.

# Works of Art

In the northern Italian town of Reggio Emilia, the childcare centers are themselves islands of beauty. The teachers' displays of children's artwork are stunningly beautiful, as is the way the rooms are arranged, free of clutter, filled with light, plants, and other objects of beauty. In addition, actual works of art, prints of famous paintings, and sculptures add islands of beauty.

You, too, can find places to display actual artwork. Begin your collection of art by obtaining prints from your local school system, library, art museum, or gallery. Or, cut prints from magazines or newspapers, and then mount and frame these.

Begin displaying art that portrays children and their families, because researchers have found that children gravitate to art that portrays children such as themselves. Choose prints of Mary Cassat's mothers and children, Rembrandt's paintings of children, or children painted by other artists.

You might set aside a space on a wall to display a work of art permanently. Think of places that need a touch of beauty. Perhaps you can hang several beautiful, calming paintings in the bathrooms, or the place where children hang their coats and store other belongings. Paintings hung in hallways also add a touch of beauty.

In addition, children enjoy postcards of famous artwork. A pack of these, with matching cards of the same print, gives children the opportunity to handle and talk about their favorite painting. Play a matching game and ask children to pick their favorite painting then find its match.

To strengthen children's awareness of the beauty around them:
- ◆ visit a local art gallery or museum
- ◆ teach children the concept of "artist"
- ◆ invite an artist to visit and sketch children
- ◆ tell children the names of the illustrators of their favorite books

**Visit a local art gallery or museum.** Do not try to go to a distant museum, but find one close to home. Often local school systems display children's artwork, and nearly every area has a gallery or local art show that would be appropriate for young children. If you only have large museums in your area, call the museum and ask to visit just one room of the museum highlighting paintings portraying children.

**Teach children the concept of "artist."** As you talk about an artist's work, describe the lines, colors, and shapes of the work and mention that the person is an *artist*—someone who creates works of art.

**Invite an artist to visit and sketch the children.** Ask children to observe the artist at work. Then they can take home their portrait.

**Tell children the names of the artists who illustrated their favorite books.** Describe how these individuals created the illustrations. For example, Leo Lionni, author of *Swimmy,* uses the technique of printing and collage to illustrate his books. Eric Carle, author of *The Very Hungry Caterpillar,* uses cut and torn paper to create collages.

After four- and five-year-olds are familiar with the name of an artist and the characteristics of his or her work, show them how to use the same technique in their own work. Look at and discuss specific works of art, perhaps before you hang these in the room. Tell children the name of the artist and something about why and how they painted as they did. Then ask children to think of a name for the painting. After they have given some names, tell them the name the painter chose. How were their ideas similar to those of the painter?

# In Summary

Every learning space for children is a place of beauty. First, necessary attention is paid to creating a clean and ordered environment. This environment is clear of clutter, but organized in ways that enable children to focus on displays and the beauty that surrounds them.

Plants and animals and other natural things enliven an environment. Children can be involved in planting their own root gardens or planting seeds. Although children should not build or clean aquariums or terrariums, they will enjoy the beauty that these bring to their classrooms. Don't forget the life outside of the room that is beautiful as well. Building and hanging a bird feeder allows children to observe the beauty of birds that come to feed.

The beauty of nature is everywhere. This beauty, whether it is found in rocks and stones, seeds, gourds, vegetables, blooming things, shells, or other items, can be displayed in ways that beautify children's rooms.

Hanging things and mobiles create other islands of beauty for children and the adults who work with them. Finally, actual works of art belong in all good schools for young children. These can be permanent or changed from time to time, and children can be taught that, they too, are artists.

# Assessing Islands of Beauty

At least once every two weeks take time to observe your room. Overall, how beautiful, calming, and ordered is your room?

Rate your room from one to five, with five being the highest, on:
- Cleanliness
  - How clean is the furniture, floor, and objects children use daily?
  - When was the last time toys and tools children used were washed with a bleach solution?
  - Orderliness
  - How organized is the room?
  - Are items on the shelves neat and ordered so children can clearly see choices?
  - When were the items on the shelves last changed?
- Elegance
  - Overall, how elegantly beautiful is the room?
  - Count the islands of beauty you find.
  - Is children's work framed and displayed?

In addition, ask yourself about:
- Growing things
  - How many plants are in the room?
  - Which need pruning? Dead leaves removed?
  - How many growing things have children planted?
- Natural things
  - Are there at least two displays in the room with any of the following natural materials?
    - Fruits/vegetables
    - Seeds/acorns
    - Gourds
    - Other
- Hanging Things
  - Are mobiles hung inside or outside for children and others to enjoy?
  - How often are these changed?
- Works of Art
  - Is there at least one work of art in the room?
  - Have you changed it in the last month?

# *Chapter* 8 Labeling Displays

Displays are not complete without labels, titles, and other written explanations. Whether these are long or short, or concise or descriptive, all must:

◆ use perfect manuscript writing that will serve as a model for children

◆ use the basics of good design

◆ serve the purpose of communicating with adults

◆ be useful for children

## Manuscript Writing

Every piece of writing that children observe serves as a model for them. In one center, after teachers read a book on how to design bulletin boards, they put dots on the ends of letters. This, the teachers decided, would "make the print prettier." Instead, it caused the young children to put dots on the letters they wrote, a practice that would have to be corrected as children progressed through school.

Take a few moments to study your own writing, knowing that children will model what you write. Look at how the letters in manuscript printing are formed from lines and circles.

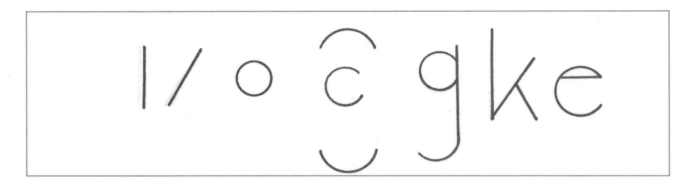

Practice manuscript writing until you perfect it and always take the time, whether writing a label on a child's painting or for a display, to write with perfection.

Aa Bb Cc Dd Ee Ff Gg
Hh Ii Jj Kk Ll Mm Nn
Oo Pp Qq Rr Ss Tt Uu Vv
Ww Xx Yy Zz

Even though it may be tempting to use all capital letters in displays as highlights, find other ways to draw attention to important labels in a display. In first grade, children will be asked to learn to use capitals only at the beginning of sentences or proper names. This is easier for them to learn if they've observed these rules in the print in their center environment.

To make it easier for you to create perfect labels, create templates of the letters or purchase templates from a school supply store. Using the template, you can readily trace and cut out perfectly formed letters.

# Design with the Basics

Labels and other written material integral to any display should follow the same basics used in creating the display. The color of the letters, their texture, shapes, and placement in the display should be considered.

### Color

Because you want children and adults alike to focus on the writing, choose bold, bright colors for lettering. For instance, if the display is a monochromatic blue tone, you might choose a bright blue for the letters, or if the display uses a neutral tone, use dark brown lettering. If your display uses complementary colors, choose one of these for the lettering. Select a color that complements the whole display, making the letters stand out from the rest of the display. Lettering can be written in any color. Often, however, black or another dark, yet neutral color is appropriate. Black printing conveys a measure of seriousness, saying this is something important—look here.

Think about the background, as well. If the background is patterned or textured, the lettering may get lost on the busy background. Placing lettering on contrasting colors helps the words stand out from the rest of the display.

### Texture

Another way to highlight letters is by cutting them from fabric. Calico, velveteen, satin, or plaid letters make a statement when used on a bulletin board or in a display. One teacher formed manuscript letters from pieces of rope to title a display about working cowhands. Another twisted sparkling wires with tiny hearts around the letters to highlight the idea that February was the "Songs of Love Month." Other teachers have covered letters with burlap, sprinkled them with sparkle dust, or created letters from wood to add texture to a display.

## Composition

Just as you arrange displays, you should arrange lettering, signs, and titles in ways that please the eye. Elements of composition include balance, symmetry, focal points, space, and rhythm. Place lettering, labels, titles, and other text asymmetrically to add interest. Remember to consider focal points of the display and use space wisely (minimize clutter!). Similar forms within a display create rhythm. Try to plan similarities between text and graphics.

### Titles

Titles should be concise and designed to attract the eye, enticing viewers to continue reading. To select concise, attractive labels first consider the display. Ask, "What is the most important point of the display?" Then think of the other "sub" points you want the display to make, if any. Write these on a piece of paper.

Now take your major point and turn it into a title for the display. Be concise. Recall how movies, magazines, and advertisements are titled. The one or two words such as *Gladiators, Friends, ER, Ebony, Essence, Woman's Day, Father of the Bride,* and so on are examples. These short, concise titles are chosen because they entice the reader to find out more.

Try to use as few words as possible. For example:
- ◆ the major point of a display following children's study of their playground might be titled "Our Playground."
- ◆ after a visit to the fire station, a display of children's drawings of their perceptions could be titled "At the Fire Station."

- a display resulting from a visit to a shoe store might be called "New Shoes, Two Shoes."
- following a visit to a clothing store, title the display, "Clothes, Clothes."

Once you decide on the title, you'll want to find an appropriate place for it in the display. On a bulletin board the title could be:
- centered (left illustration)
- asymmetrical (right illustration)

In a display, a title could be mounted on a triangular frame.

Or it could be placed in a stand holder.

### Subtitles

Often you'll need subtitles to make the total display more meaningful. Using the sub ideas of the display you've previously identified, create subtitles. For example:
- subtitles for a display about the play yard could be: "How Many Climbers Do We Have?" "I Can Slide," and "We Ride Our Bikes."
- subtitles for a display of the visit to the fire station could consist of "Jobs Firefighters Do," " Where Firefighters Sleep," or "The Fire Truck."
- subtitles for a display of a visit to the shoe store could be "Which Do You Choose?" "Shoes with Strings, Velcro, and Buckles," and "Dress-Up Shoes."

◆ to help children make sense of a visit to the clothing store, use subtitles such as "T-Shirts," "Jeans," Clothes We Like," or "Clothes for Teenagers."

# Communicate with Adults

## Displays

Some displays are prepared for adults. Other teachers in the school, parents, visitors to the school, and school administrators can learn a lot from displays of children's work or displays constructed only for them. These, too, require labels. Labels serve to entice adults to focus on the display. A well-posed question, statement, or problem can involve adults as participating members of the display. Because the major purpose is to communicate information to parents, a plain background with black printing of viewable size is recommended.

Adults read the labels and narratives in a display to:
◆ understand what children are doing and learning
◆ learn about child growth, development, and learning
◆ document what children have learned
◆ learn how children make friends, cooperate, and share
◆ learn songs, rhymes, and poetry
◆ understand how children learn to write
◆ comprehend how children think and solve problems

**Understand what children are doing and learning.** Labeling and narratives tell adults something of the context in which the work took place. This context tells adults what led children to this work, how children went about completing the work, and what they said and did.

**Learn about child growth, development, and learning.** Even though parents are experts about their own children, they may not know a lot about typical child growth and development. Labeling children's artwork and describing what children did gives parents and other adults who visit the school information about how children typically progress from scribbling to writing, or from recognizing rhyming words to reading, and it describes and explains children's experiences and work. Labels that describe the stages of children's art development, how language develops, or children's mathematical and scientific development inform parents and other adults.

**How children make friends, cooperate, and share.** Along with photos of children engaged in everyday work and play, write narratives describing the social skills that the children have learned, such as cooperating, sharing, waiting for a turn, and listening and working with others.

**How children learn songs, rhymes, and poetry.** Display copies of the poems, songs, and rhymes that the children have learned. Write a narrative of what this means for children's reading readiness. Knowing rhymes, being able to point out rhyming words, is an essential step in phonemic awareness.

**How children learn to write.** Display early samples of children's scribbles and compare these to current writing samples. You might use samples from a previous year so parents and children will not be able to compare or compete with each other. Use a narrative to describe how children learn to write.

**How children think and solve problems.** Using photographs and children's work samples, describe how children solved problems for themselves. Document the thinking process by labeling photos and children's experiences as "observing," "collecting information," "analyzing data," and "reaching conclusions."

### Children's Work

Labeling children's work helps to communicate the progress children are making or what their drawing, painting, invented spelling, or other work means. You can write a description of what the child's work means on the back of the work or the back of a frame. When displaying this child's work, copy his or her description and place it underneath the displayed work. Or, you might tell what the child was doing or saying at the time a painting was created.

Labels might also explain the child's development and progress. Knowing something of the typical stages of the development of drawing and writing helps parents appreciate children's early work.

You might use labels:
- when children gain control over scribbling, beginning to close scribbles and repeat forms.
- to point out children's first attempts at writing found in their scribbles.

"I am learning to write"    Juan /May 2

- to let parents know that children drawing a circle to represent a figure is the beginning of symbolic thought.

## Communicate Information

Sometimes displays are created for the sole purpose of communicating information to parents. These displays are placed at adults' eye level in places not used by children. Through print and pictures, these displays might communicate:
- the bus schedule and routines
- the classroom schedule
- tips on packing nutritious lunches
- new and interesting books for children or parents

# Useful for Children

Children, who are just learning that print conveys meaning, need to find their work labeled. Some displays require a simple title. Other boards or labels can be labeled with questions, explanations, narratives, or directions. Regardless, the labels should:

- ◆ tell children something new,
- ◆ give children something to observe,
- ◆ give children something to do,
- ◆ describe something children should know, or
- ◆ help children reflect on past experiences.

## Tell Children Something New

"Look, look," said five-year-old Sasha, running to a table display, "It's a frog, it's a frog." The teacher had added a frog to the class terrarium and placed the terrarium on a table, along with the sign, "Look! Look! What's New?"

Even before children are able to read, signs inform them of something new to examine or observe. This technique can also be used with something that is not new to the room or even the children. Teachers have drawn children's attention to games, toys, or other objects that they have forgotten by highlighting them in a display.

You might use a label or title to draw children's attention to:

- ◆ a new board game for the room
- ◆ a book that has been forgotten
- ◆ a new piece of equipment for the playground, perhaps a ball, trike, or other object
- ◆ packets of seeds to plant inside or outside
- ◆ an object related to a poem or story children know. One teacher received a gift of salt and pepper shakers in the form of Humpty Dumpty. She drew children's attention to the shakers with a label that said, "Humpty Dumpty Is Here." After examining and playing with the shakers, children reenacted the rhyme.

### Give Children Something to Observe

To foster children's observation skills, throughout the year teachers give children things to observe. Labels or signs, even when teachers read them to children, inform them.

Signs can alert children to observe:

◆ Chrysalises developing—Encourage children to check the chrysalis and notice when changes occur by posting a sign that says, "Watch the Chrysalis Each Day." This may enable children to observe the butterfly emerging.

◆ Worm tunnels—Place the sign "Worms at Work" on a large, plastic jar covered with black paper that holds a colony of worms. Remove the paper so the children can observe worms tunneling and working. Use "Ants at Work" for a similar jar holding ants.

◆ Snails—The sign "How Many Snails Can You Find?" asks children to try to count the snails in the aquarium.

### Give Children Something to Do

The question, "What Color Can You Make?" asks children to experiment with mixing paints. Supply plastic cups and clear squirt bottles holding red, yellow, and blue paint and instruct children to squirt two colors into a cup to find out what colors they can make.

Throughout the year other signs can inform children to:

◆ "Write a Letter" at a table containing stationery, envelopes, markers, and stamps.

◆ "Play a Game" using the board games in the classroom.

◆ "Make Some Music" with a display of a triangle, sand blocks, and tonal blocks.

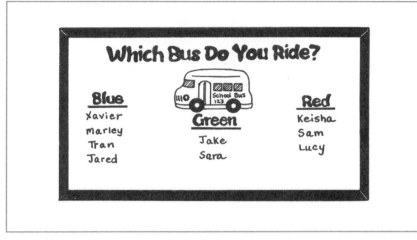

- ◆ "Read a Book" at a table of new library books.
- ◆ "Finish a Puzzle" as directed by a sign on a table displaying a few puzzles.

## Describe Something Children Should Know

Signs and labels, along with pictures, photos, and other explanations are used to inform children of:
- ◆ a change in the schedule
- ◆ what they'll have for snack
- ◆ which bus to ride
- ◆ a special event
- ◆ where to ride bikes

## Help Children Reflect on Past Experiences

Displaying what children have completed gives them an opportunity to reflect on and recall past experiences. These displays can be labeled in ways that prompt children's thinking or help them summarize and reach conclusions about an experience.

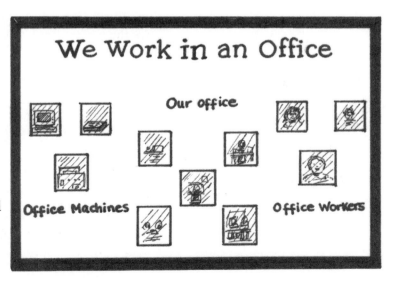

For example, after a theme on office workers, a display of photos of parents or others working in an office could include pictures and a list of office machines that children observed titled, "Office Machines." Another section of photos might be labeled "Office Workers," and still another area of the display could be titled "Our Office," with photos of the children playing "office."

Displaying photos of children shopping and the clothing they saw following a visit to a clothing store helps children recall their visit. Or, after finishing a theme on musical instruments, display photos of children playing classroom instruments and photos of musicians playing real instruments.

## In Summary

Labels are an important part of any display. Labels inform and communicate the meaning of the display and children's work. Some labels are designed for adults and others for children's use. All labels should be created using manuscript writing because they will serve as models for children as they begin to write and invent their own spelling.

Consider the basics of design, using color, form, texture, and composition when creating labels. Most labels will be in black or other bright or dark colors to help them stand out. Using neutral backgrounds also helps labels stand out from the rest of the display. Choose concise titles and subtitles to draw attention to the display and make the display more useful.

Labels and displays designed for parents communicate what children are doing and learning during the day as well as convey important information to parents, such as changes in schedules or to confirm procedures. Labels for children tell them something new, give them something they can observe, give them something to do, describe something they need to know, or help them reflect or think about past experiences.

## Assessing Labeling

Before you finish creating a display, ask if the labels on the display:
- ◆ are in perfect manuscript writing, with capitals and lower-case letters used appropriately?
- ◆ stand out from the rest of the display?
- ◆ are large enough and dark enough to call children's and adult's attention to the display?

Now look at your titles and assess them. Are they:
- ◆ concise? In a word or two, do they convey the central meaning of the display?
- ◆ highlighted in the display? Are they placed symmetrically or asymmetrically to break up the display, and at the same time, convey the sub-meanings of the display?

Read the narratives that you include in your display and ask if these:
- ◆ communicate to parents or other adults in the program? Do they tell what children did, why they did it, and what the goals of the experience were?
- ◆ inform parents of children's progress and learning?
- ◆ communicate important information?

Look at the narratives and labels you want children to use. Ask yourself if these use words children know and inform them of something new, to observe, do, or think about?

When you first display the work, observe how many children and adults gravitate to the display, look at it, and talk about it. Keep track of how many continue to use the display. When children and adults no longer find the display of interest, then change it.

# Resources
## and References

## Resources

Brown-DuPaul, J., T. Keyes, and L. Segatti. 2001. Using documentation panels to communicate with families. *Childhood Education,* 77, 204-208.

Coleman, M., & C. Wallinga. 2000. Connecting families and classrooms using family involvement webs. *Childhood Education,76,* 209-214.

Cooper, H., P. Hegarty, P. Hegarty, & N. Simco. 1996. *Display in the classroom.* London: David Fulton Publishers.

Helm, J. H., S. Beneke, & K. Steinheimer. 1998. *Windows on learning: Documenting young children's work.* New York: Teachers College Press.

Herr, J., & Y. Libby. 1997. *Creative resources for bulletin boards in the early childhood classroom.* Beltsville, MD: Gryphon House.

Meagher, J. & J. Novelli. 1998. *Interactive bulletin boards: Language arts.* New York: Scholastic.

National Association for the Education of Young Children 1996. NAEYC position statement: Responding to linguistic and cultural diversity-Recommendations for effective early childhood education. *Young Children,* 51 (2), 4-12.

# References

Aliki 1982. *We are best friends.* New York: Mulberry Paperback Books.

Carle, E. 1988. *Do you want to be my friend?* New York: Putnam Publishing Group.

Carle, E. 1969. *The very hungry caterpillar.* New York: The World Publishing House.

Field, E. 1996. *Wynken, Blyken and Nod.* New York: North/South Books.

Fleming, A. 1999. *In the small, small pond.* New York: Econo Clad Books.

Fleming, A. 1995. *In the tall, tall grass.* New York: Holt.

Johnson, C. 1999. *Harold and the purple crayon.* New York: Econo Clad Books

Lionni, L. 1992. *Swimmy.* New York: Knopf.

Milne, A. A. 1992. *Now we are six.* New York: Puffin.

Rogers, F. 1996. *Making friends.* New York: Paper Star.

Rossetti, C. 1997. What is pink? In C. Rossetti's *Everyman* paperback classics. New York: Everyman Classics.

Sendak, M. 1963. *Where the wild things are.* New York: Harper Collins.

Shaw, C.G. 1999. *It looked like spilt milk.* New York: Celebration Press.

# Index

# Playing to Learn
### Activities and Experiences that Build Learning Connections
*Carol Seefeldt*

*Playing to Learn* gives you hundreds of activities, games, and experiences to make learning fun, through games, small group activities, stories, and more. Each chapter includes activities that connect different areas of the curriculum, assessment and evaluation tools, and ways to extend learning by connecting home and school. Designed to match children's development, these activities promote learning on any kind of day—from a hot and sunny day to a wet and rainy day; when you have to wait, when everyone is sad and blue, and when there is nothing to do!  192 pages. 2001.

**ISBN 0-87659-263-9 / Gryphon House / 19325 / Paperback**

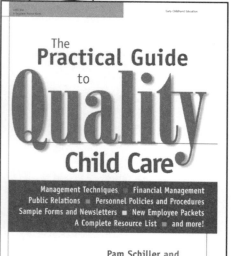

# The Practical Guide to Quality Child Care
*Pam Schiller and Patricia Carter Dyke*

This uniquely comprehensive manual is a clear, easy-to-read handbook that provides specific guidelines for virtually every aspect of early childhood administration. Contents include sample forms, procedures for program development, schedules, applications, and evaluations. An invaluable tool for every child care facility manager. 192 pages. 2001.

**ISBN 0-87659-262-0 / Gryphon House / 17356 / Paperback**

Available at your favorite bookstore, school supply store, or order from Gryphon House at 800.638.0928 or www.gryphonhouse.com.

## Early Learning Environments That Work

*Rebecca Isbell and Betty Exelby*

*Early Learning Environments That Work* explores how you can work with furniture, color, materials, storage, lighting, and more to encourage learning through classroom arrangement. 192 pages. 2001.

**ISBN 0-87659-256-6 / Gryphon House / 14387 / Paperback**

## The Portfolio Book
A Step-by-Step Guide for Teachers

*Elizabeth F. Shores and*

*Cathy Grace*

*The Portfolio Book* introduces a method to help early childhood teachers improve the responsiveness of their teaching. The 10-step guide breaks the portfolio assessment process into small, easy-to-manage steps that can be integrated painlessly into everyday teaching. 192 pages. 1998.

**ISBN 0-87659-194-2 / Gryphon House / 15468 / Paperback**

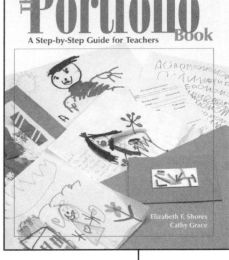

🏆 • Benjamin Franklin Award

## MathArts

Exploring Math Through Art for
3 to 6 Year Olds

*MaryAnn F. Kohl and Cindy Gainer*

Get ready to create and count in an exciting
introduction to math that uses creative art
projects to introduce early math concepts.
Each of the 200 hands-on projects is designed
to help children discover essential math skills
through a creative process unique to every
individual. The possibilities are endless!
256 pages. 1996.

**ISBN 0-87659-177-2 / Gryphon House**

**16987 / Paperback**

## Cooking Art

Easy Edible Art for Young Children

*MaryAnn F. Kohl and Jean Potter*

Transform the classroom into an artist's studio with these easy
edible art experiences. *Cooking Art* combines the familiar area
of art exploration with the fascinating world of cooking,
including all of its wondrous tools, tastes, and outcomes.
Includes recipes for snacks, sandwiches, drinks, desserts,
breads, fruit, and pet treats. 192 pages. 1997.

**ISBN 0-87659-184-5 / Gryphon House / 18237 / Paperback**

> ♆ • Early Childhood News Director's Award
> • Parent Council Award

**Available at your
favorite bookstore,
school supply store,
or order from Gryphon House
at 800.638.0928 or
www.gryphonhouse.com.**

## Preschool Art

It's the Process, Not the Product

*MaryAnn F. Kohl*

Over 200 activities encourage children to
explore and understand their world through
art experiences that emphasize the process of
art, not the product. The first chapter
introduces basic art activities appropriate for all
children, while the subsequent chapters, which build on the basic activities in
the first chapter, are divided by seasons. Activities are included for painting,
drawing, collage, sculpture, and construction. Indexes organized by art medium
and project name help teachers plan. 260 pages. 1994.

**ISBN 0-87659-168-3 / Gryphon House / 16985 / Paperback**

- Benjamin Franklin Award
- Early Childhood News Director's Award

## The Big Messy* Art Book

*But Easy to Clean Up

*MaryAnn F. Kohl*

Adventurous art beyond your wildest
imagination! Combine the joy of creativity,
the delight of imagination, and the thrill of
an art adventure. *The Big Messy Art Book*
opens the door for children to explore art on
a grander, more expressive scale. Paint a one-
of-a-kind masterpiece from a swing, or try painting a hanging
ball while it moves! With *The Big Messy Art Book,* you are giving
children the opportunity to go beyond the ordinary and into the
amazing! 135 pages. 2000.

**ISBN 0-87659-206-X / Gryphon House / 14925 / Paperback**

- Early Childhood News Director's Award

# The Complete Daily Curriculum for Early Childhood

Over 1200 Easy Activities to Support Multiple Intelligences and Learning Styles

*Pam Schiller and Pat Phipps*

This innovative book for three- to six-year-olds offers a complete plan for every learning style. Organized by theme, *The Complete Daily Curriculum* includes a morning circle and end-of-day reflection, and different activities for each learning center. With over 1,200 activities and ideas to engage multiple intelligences, plus assessment tools and a comprehensive appendix of songs, stories, games, dances, props, recipes, patterns, chants, rhymes, and arts and crafts, you'll find everything you need to captivate and challenge every child in your classroom. 608 pages. 2002.

**ISBN 0-87659-228-0 / Gryphon House / 16279 / Paperback**

# The Complete Learning Center Book

An Illustrated Guide for 32 Different
Early Childhood Learning Centers

*Rebecca Isbell*

Enrich your classroom with unique learning centers and new ideas for traditional centers. Clear illustrations provide a layout of each center with suggestions for setting up the classroom environment. Each section includes an introduction, learning objectives, a letter to parents, related vocabulary, and a web of integrated learning that diagrams the range of curriculum areas taught. All you need to know about these 32 learning centers is included in this comprehensive book. 365 pages. 1995.

**ISBN 0-87659-174-8 / Gryphon House / 17584 / Paperback**

**Available at your favorite bookstore, school supply store, or order from Gryphon House at 800.638.0928 or www.gryphonhouse.com.**

## Prop Box Play

### 50 Themes to Inspire Dramatic Play

*Ann Barbour and Blanche Desjean-Perrotta*

Think inside the (prop) box! Encourage more dramatic play with *Prop Box Play.* Prop boxes contain dramatic play props that offer children the freedom to express themselves and to exercise their imaginations. Props that inspire children to play different roles (archeologist, veterinarian, undersea explorer) help them interact with each other, cultivating important social skills. With 50 themes that inspire hours of dramatic play and creativity, lists of props, easy extensions, related vocabulary, and associated children's literature, *Prop Box Play* makes it easy for children to bring their imaginations to life! 160 pages. 2002.

**ISBN 0-87659-277-9 / Gryphon House / 13615 / Paperback**

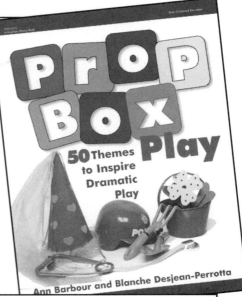

## Block Play

### The Complete Guide to Learning and Playing with Blocks

*Sharon MacDonald*

Create craft-board trees, railroad tracks and skyscrapers, and watch children experience the joy of learning through blocks! Each activity includes clear descriptions of what children learn, and encourages developmental skills such as problem-solving, math, science, language, and social skills. *Block Play* is a must-have for every teacher. 192 pages. 2001.

**ISBN 0-87659-253-1 / Gryphon House / 19327 / Paperback**

🏆 • Early Childhood News Director's Award

Available at your favorite bookstore, school supply store, or order from Gryphon House at 800.638.0928 or www.gryphonhouse.com.

# The GIANT Encyclopedia of Theme Activities for Children 2 to 5

Over 600 Favorite Activities Created by Teachers for Teachers

*Edited by Kathy Charner*

This popular potpourri of over 600 classroom-tested activities actively engages children's imaginations and provides many months of learning fun. Organized into 48 popular themes, from dinosaurs to circuses to outer space, these favorites are the result of a nationwide competition. 511 pages. 1993.

**ISBN 0-87659-166-7 / Gryphon House / 19216 / Paperback**

# The GIANT Encyclopedia of Circle Time and Group Activities for Children 3 to 6

Over 600 Favorite Circle Time Activities
Created by Teachers for Teachers

*Edited by Kathy Charner*

Open to any page in this book and you will find an activity for circle or group time written by an experienced teacher. Filled with over 600 activities covering 48 themes, this book is jam-packed with ideas that were tested by teachers in the classroom. 510 pages. 1996.

**ISBN 0-87659-181-0 / Gryphon House / 16413 / Paperback**

**Available at your favorite bookstore, school supply store, or order from Gryphon House at 800.638.0928 or www.gryphonhouse.com.**

# The GIANT Encyclopedia of Art & Craft Activities for Children 3 to 6

More Than 500 Art & Craft Activities
Written by Teachers for Teachers

*Edited by Kathy Charner*

A comprehensive collection of the best art and craft activities for young children. Teacher-created, classroom-tested art activities to actively engage children's imaginations! The result of a nationwide competition, these art and craft activities are the best of the best. Just the thing to add pizzazz to your day! 568 pages. 2000.

**ISBN 0-87659-209-4 / Gryphon House / 16854 / Paperback**

# The GIANT Encyclopedia of Science Activities for Children 3 to 6

More Than 600 Science Activities
Written by Teachers for Teachers

*Edited by Kathy Charner*

Leave your fears of science behind as our *GIANT Encyclopedia* authors have done. Respond to children's natural curiosity with over 600 teacher-created, classroom-tested activities guaranteed to teach your children about science while they are having fun. 575 pages. 1998.

**ISBN 0-87659-193-4 / Gryphon House / 18325 / Paperback**